# Unfinished

Published by Barbour Books, an imprint of Barbour Publishing, Inc., 1810 Barbour Drive, Uhrichsville, Ohio 44683, www.barbourbooks.com

*Our mission is to inspire the world with the life-changing message of the Bible.*

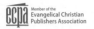
Member of the
Evangelical Christian
Publishers Association

Printed in China.

# Unfinished

## Devotions & Prayers for a Heart Under Construction

### Linda Hang

BARBOUR BOOKS
An Imprint of Barbour Publishing, Inc.

# Introduction

We are unfinished—like a sentence without a period, like a building with the scaffolding still up. God hasn't finished constructing us. From the moment we believe in Him—really, before then when He calls us to Himself—He is working in our hearts. Our every moment as a Christian He is crafting us in faith, in love, in wisdom, in peace, in holiness. . .until the moment we reach heaven.

And we may wonder why. Why not redeem us and perfect us in one fell swoop? He could do it. During the rapture, believers will be changed "in the twinkling of an eye" (1 Corinthians 15:52). Why not now? Whatever God's ultimate reason, He chooses to shape us bit by bit. He chooses to build up our hearts little by little. He chooses to work in our lives day by day.

Truly, God is the one shaping, building, working. He is the power behind the process, and we never need to doubt His presence. Come rain or shine, trials or blessings, bad days or good, He is with us.

So turn the page and start exploring the ways God is present and at work *in you.* But these devotions just skim the surface. May God use them to inspire you to go deeper into His Word and to meet with Him daily as you. . .

*With unveiled face, beholding as in a mirror
the glory of the Lord, are being transformed
into the same image from glory to glory.*
2 CORINTHIANS 3:18 NKJV

5

# Just a Preview

*Beloved, we are God's children now, and what we will be has not yet appeared; but we know that when he appears we shall be like him, because we shall see him as he is.*

1 JOHN 3:2

She looked at the packet of seeds in her hand. On the outside was a picture of beautiful flowers; on the inside was a sprinkling of tiny brown pellets. She went to work—breaking up the soil, planting the seeds, watering the earth. When she was done, she sat back on her heels and smiled. In her mind she saw the flowers as they would one day be.

The Christian life is a little like those seeds. Once we believe in Jesus, God adopts us into His family. We are children of God, heirs with Christ (Romans 8:17), but we're not exactly like God's perfect Son yet. God still has some work to do as He grows us into the likeness of Jesus. Through the process, though, we have the hope of glorified lives in heaven. Think on these words from the apostle Paul:

> *The body is sown in corruption, it is raised in incorruption. It is sown in dishonor, it is raised in glory. It is sown in weakness, it is raised in power. It is sown a natural body, it is raised a spiritual body. There is a natural body, and there is a spiritual body. And so it is written,*

*"The first man Adam became a living being."*
*The last Adam became a life-giving spirit.*

*However, the spiritual is not first, but the natural, and afterward the spiritual. The first man was of the earth, made of dust; the second Man is the Lord from heaven. As was the man of dust, so also are those who are made of dust; and as is the heavenly Man, so also are those who are heavenly. And as we have borne the image of the man of dust, we shall also bear the image of the heavenly Man.*
(1 Corinthians 15:42–49 NKJV)

What is our role as we await His appearing and the moment we will be like Him? "Since we have these promises, beloved, let us cleanse ourselves from every defilement of body and spirit, bringing holiness to completion in the fear of God" (2 Corinthians 7:1). God has begun something beautiful in us, and He will finish it one day. Guaranteed. In the meantime, the promise fills us with so much anticipation that we can't wait for heaven to be like Him. So we start now.

*Father, to be like Your Son—I can only imagine what that will be like! Help me to be more and more like Him even now. Amen.*

# Lead Your Life

*Only let each person lead the life that the Lord has assigned to him, and to which God has called him.*

1 Corinthians 7:17

**S**ocial media. Do you love it? Do you hate it? With it we can keep tabs on family members and friends; we can laugh, cheer, and share with others. On the flip side, it can also become a black hole of comparison. We know "all about" a college friend's engagement. We see hundreds of congrats and well wishes when another friend has twins. We get a play-by-play of a neighbor's remodel. We hear about job promotions, vacations, Zumba classes, parties (that we may or may not have been invited to). . . While each of these things is good, if we're honest, can't social media sometimes be a drag, especially when we find our lives looking slightly dull next to all the shine in someone else's life? If we aren't careful, we can start to yearn for blessings that aren't ours to enjoy, to desire a life that isn't ours to walk.

Each time you use social media, remember Paul's words in his letter to the Corinthian church. Paul advised believers to be content in whatever state they were in—whether married, unmarried, circumcised, uncircumcised, slave, or free. Like a horse wearing blinders, the Corinthians were to "lead the life" God had for them, without being distracted looking to the left or the right at what others were doing or being swayed to think they were inadequate in their current state.

God crafts and blesses the best life for every one of His children. Yet in His amazing, boundless love and wisdom, He blesses and leads each of His children in a unique way. He cares about *you* individually. He has a plan for *your* life distinctly. You are not one in a numberless crowd. You are [fill in your name]. And as long as you still breathe in and out, He's not finished guiding you down your life's path. He's not finished blessing you as only He knows how.

Don't let social media drag you down! The next time envy or discontentment pops up, when the devil whispers that God isn't present in your life the way He is in everybody else's, cry out to God for blinders to see the road He's placed you on. Like a horse confidently clip-clopping along the road, have faith in your heavenly Father's ability to call you to the perfect path, to bless you in exactly the right way.

*Father, You know the beginning and the end.*
*I rest in You and Your plans for me, believing*
*You'll see them through. Amen.*

# The Road Ahead

*But, as it is written, "What no eye has seen,
nor ear heard, nor the heart of man imagined, what
God has prepared for those who love him."*
1 Corinthians 2:9

If you've ever stood at a figurative crossroads in your life, you probably know what it's like to need wisdom. Which direction? Which choice? The "roads" stretch out in front of you, wide open, but you're unsure which to take. They both continue beyond sight, but you can't begin to see which one is best. The not knowing paralyzes you, preventing you from moving at all. *What if I make the wrong decision, go the wrong way?* you ask.

When we feel stalled, God is still moving. And He's preparing the directions if only we'll ask and allow the Holy Spirit to answer. In fact, what He has for us is beyond anything we've seen, heard, or imagined.

Sounds amazing! But waiting on His direction is not so easy, is it? It can be pretty difficult.

The problem is focusing on God when this life demands our attention. (It's always around us, bumping into us, after all.) The problem is trusting God when we've been told to rely on ourselves. (We're self-made women—hear us roar!) The problem is waiting on God when we desperately want a solution *now*. (Instant download, please.) The problem is believing in something we have not seen, heard, or imagined.

The good news is this: Our God is absolutely able and more than willing to help us with these problems. He has not left us to struggle on our own; He has equipped us with the Holy Spirit. "Now we have received not the spirit of the world, but the Spirit who is from God, that we might understand the things freely given us by God" (1 Corinthians 2:12). If you are His child, God's Spirit is alive within you, working to illuminate His Word, shedding light on the way ahead.

Keeping an open mind to all God has in store isn't always easy; it takes faith. But each moment you choose to exercise faith strengthens your faith. Like muscle memory, our eyes become sharpened to see His hand at work, our ears become attuned to hear His voice, our hearts become conditioned to hope in Him. At that crossroads, take comfort in the words of Isaiah: "And your ears shall hear a word behind you, saying, 'This is the way, walk in it,' when you turn to the right or when you turn to the left" (Isaiah 30:21).

*Lord, I feel so alone standing here at this crossroads.*
*Hold my hand. Lead me, please. I choose today to*
*believe that You can provide understanding*
*beyond anything I can conceive. Amen.*

# On the Way

*While I was speaking in prayer, the man Gabriel,*
*whom I had seen in the vision at the first, came to me in*
*swift flight at the time of the evening sacrifice. He made me*
*understand, speaking with me and saying, "O Daniel, I have*
*now come out to give you insight and understanding. At the*
*beginning of your pleas for mercy a word went out, and I*
*have come to tell it to you, for you are greatly loved."*
DANIEL 9:21–23

ilence—what with alarms, traffic, lawn mowers, music at gas pumps, ringtones, toddlers, sirens, and the list goes on, we all crave a little peace and quiet at times. But there's one area of our lives where we usually never want to hear silence: our prayers. God's silence is deadening. In that silence, we can easily forget that God hears our prayers and that He's at work answering them.

Did you catch the first words of Daniel 9:21? *"While I was speaking. . ."* Daniel hadn't finished praying, and Gabriel appeared. So when he began praying, or even before, God heard and sent an answer. Isaiah says of God, "Before they call I will answer; while they are yet speaking I will hear" (Isaiah 65:24). Our God is not too distant to hear the faintest voice; He is not too busy to handle one more request or listen to one more word. He is our heavenly Father, caring and close, so much so that He knows what we need even before we ask it (Matthew 6:8).

Today, wherever you need encouragement, boldness,

resources; whatever your desires, thoughts, troubles—you name it—God knows your heart. Don't hold back, but approach your Father in openness and humility. Gabriel's message to Daniel included the why of God's answer: "for you are greatly loved." God anticipates, hears, and answers His children's prayers because we are greatly loved. *You* are greatly loved. When your prayers seem to disintegrate before they reach the ceiling, let alone heaven, say the words to yourself (it's okay if you feel silly!): *I am greatly loved.* Rest in His love. Rest in the knowledge that He is awesome enough to answer prayers before they are prayed.

How many times do we think of God in heaven listening to our words and then saying, *"Hmm, interesting. I'll give that some thought and get back to you"*? Deeper than faith that God will respond, let's begin to have faith that He is working even while we are still speaking.

*Father, I bow my head today in awe of who You are. You hear every prayer. Fill me with assurance in the silence that You have been and are at work. Amen.*

# It's a Promise!

*And I am sure of this, that he who began a good work in you will bring it to completion at the day of Jesus Christ.*

PHILIPPIANS 1:6

Have you ever met anyone who leaves things unfinished? (Maybe you're among the ranks of the start-but-don't-finish-ers.) A hand-knitted sock that has no mate. A novel deserted halfway through. Clean laundry left in the basket. The pristine gardening supplies on a shelf. Beginnings aren't always hard, but following through can be tough, especially when we get tired, discouraged, distracted, or busy.

While being a finisher isn't all-important in every aspect of life (that gym membership might not have been the greatest idea anyway), when it comes to what really matters, we're glad when we, and others, finish what we start. You'd be in trouble if your mechanic did only half an oil change. You'd be upset if you worked all week and your boss didn't pay you. You'd be disappointed in yourself if you bailed on plans with a friend for no good reason, or filled out but never submitted your tax return, or never achieved a dream. Finishing equals completion, closure. It's the well-earned sigh that comes at the end of a task, big or small.

When you believed in Jesus, your faith journey began. Since then God has been at work, transforming you to be more like His Son. For now we're unfinished. But with all the ups and downs of growing in Christ, the end, your salvation, is secure. Paul wrote in Colossians 3:3–4, "For you have died, and your life is *hidden* with Christ in God. When Christ who is your life appears, then you also will appear with him in glory" (emphasis added). And again Paul wrote, "In him you also, when you heard the word of truth, the gospel of your salvation, and believed in him, were *sealed* with the promised Holy Spirit, who is the *guarantee* of our inheritance until we acquire possession of it, to the praise of his glory" (Ephesians 1:13–14, emphasis added). Think about those words: *hidden*—kept safe from harm; *sealed*—no one can alter it; *guarantee*—for certain.

Surrounded by what's yet unfinished in this life, we may naturally feel uncertain. But whether God will finish what He has begun isn't up in the air. He is faithful. He did not give us the promise of eternal life only to leave loose ends, the job half done. Having sacrificed His Son, God will not stop short of salvation. He "will bring it to completion."

*God, forgive me for doubting You. You're forever faithful, and You'll not leave unfinished what You've started. Thank You for salvation, now and for always in heaven. Amen.*

# For Our Good

*And we know that for those who love God all things*
*work together for good, for those who are*
*called according to his purpose.*
ROMANS 8:28

M aybe you have experienced a lot of rough waters in your
life. You're a survivor; you've endured what many people
couldn't imagine. But even if just a few hardships have come your
way, or tons of "little" things have plagued your steps, you might
find yourself scratching your head after reading Paul's words in
Romans 8:28. *"All things. . .for good." Really, Paul? Even cancer,*
*violence, natural disasters. . . ? This world is so very broken.*
*Everything can't eventually lead to sunshine and buttercups.*

Take a moment to think about Paul's life. After a miraculous
conversion to Christianity, Paul went through tough times. He
was falsely accused, beaten, imprisoned, and shipwrecked, to
name a few. He was no stranger to suffering, both in his life and
in the lives of those he loved. Yet he was also confident that God
had good plans in and through the bad.

How can we adopt this optimism when life brings us to our
knees, and sometimes beats us into the ground? By looking up.

Just before his words of encouragement, Paul wrote, "For
I consider that the sufferings of this present time are not worth
comparing with the glory that is to be revealed to us" (Romans
8:18). There's so much *more* to come. By fixing our minds on

heaven (Colossians 3:2), we as Christians realize that our lives don't end with our last breath on earth. Eternity awaits. God is working everything for good—in our earthly lives as well as our heavenly ones.

And there's so much *more* that God is working to accomplish. God is a big God; He has big plans. With our eyes focused on Him, we aren't so likely to see life centered in and revolving around us, but rather coming from God and for His glory. We aren't so likely to forget the One who commands the whole picture: "I am God, and there is none like me, declaring the end from the beginning and from ancient times things not yet done" (Isaiah 46:9–10). All of what God has in mind for His children we can't begin to fathom, but we can begin to have faith that what He has in mind is good.

So even while being battered by the winds, don't lose sight of the horizon. Blue sky is hidden behind those stormy clouds, just waiting for God to reveal it.

*Lord, You turn sorrow into joy, weakness into strength, bad into good. You are amazing! Increase my faith that You are working all things for good. Amen.*

# The B-I-B-L-E

*All Scripture is breathed out by God and profitable for teaching, for reproof, for correction, and for training in righteousness, that the man of God may be complete.*
2 TIMOTHY 3:16–17

What is the Bible? To some, the Bible is a history book. To others, a collection of stories. To Christians, the Bible is so much more. It is the Word of God, and through it He speaks to believers.

How you view the Bible can make a tremendous difference in how you approach reading it. If Bible reading becomes just another item on a to-do list, our eyes will take in the words but those words won't reach deep inside. We'll miss an opportunity to grow in our faith. But if instead we begin our quiet times inviting God to speak through His Word, He will. By opening our Bibles with a willingness to hear, we'll open the door to a powerful source of wisdom: "For the word of God is living and active, sharper than any two-edged sword, piercing to the division of soul and of spirit, of joints and of marrow, and discerning the thoughts and intentions of the heart" (Hebrews 4:12). Unlike any other book in print, out of print, or yet to be printed, the Bible transforms us in real, lasting, to-our-core ways. Paul likely was thinking about the radical results of God's Word when he wrote to the Thessalonians, "And we also thank God constantly for this, that when you received the word of God, which you heard from us, you accepted it not as the word of men but as what it really is, the word of God, which is at work in you believers" (1 Thessalonians 2:13).

That same Word of God is at work in believers still, deepening their faith as they grow more Christlike day by day. So wherever you need God's hand in your life, open your Bible. Make Bible reading as essential to you as the oxygen that flows into your lungs with every breath.

Maybe you feel distant from God. Maybe it has been a while since you've dusted off the cover of your Bible, or maybe personal Bible study has never been a part of your daily routine. When you begin to read, the words. . .are just words. Don't give up. Pray. Let God know how you're feeling—your frustration, your desire to hear, your need for His help.

God gave us His Word for a reason. As we do our small part in the process, He is faithful to work in us.

*Lord, Your Word is powerful, and I want to experience that power for myself. Open my spiritual eyes as I open the Bible and read. Amen.*

# Unplanned Stop

*"For as the heavens are higher than the earth, so are my ways higher than your ways and my thoughts than your thoughts."*
Isaiah 55:9

Picture this: A lonely road out in the middle of nowhere, both ends extending far into the distance. You stand beside your car, which is pulled off to the side where it limped to a halt. You're stranded. Temporarily stuck between points A and B. Imagine that this is an unexpected event on a carefully planned road trip. For weeks, maybe months, you pored over maps and guidebooks, meticulously plotting the route you'd take, the places you'd stop. You might have spent years dreaming of a trip just like this and where you'd end up. . .except, of course, for this moment. When will you be on your way again? Will you have to make a detour? Will you reach your destination at all?

Now apply this scenario to your life's journey. Do you feel stalled somewhere? Were you hoping to earn a college degree but you've had to put your education on hold? Did you think you'd be married by now? Have you been praying for a child for years? There are lots of places where we can feel stuck. No matter how long we've dreamed, planned, worked, or prayed, sometimes we're going nowhere fast. Where we've been is behind us, and where we want to be is still out of reach.

In these moments, it's easy to forget that with all the dreaming and planning, working and praying, God is ultimately in control.

Proverbs 16:9 says, "The heart of man plans his way, but the Lord establishes his steps." Yet even if we wholeheartedly yield to God's road map for our lives, we still may wonder what He's up to. We perceive no purpose in the in-between—but God does. He sees what's taking place in our lives from the heights; He understands what's going on with a depth unreachable to us without Him. As the words of Isaiah proclaim, His ways are higher, His thoughts are higher, so much higher than our own.

For whatever reason, God has you here now. Standing on the roadside of life, remember: you're not stranded forever and without purpose. Your great and loving Lord is the one who said, "For I know the plans I have for you. . .plans for welfare and not for evil, to give you a future and a hope" (Jeremiah 29:11). He holds the itinerary. Can you trust Him?

*God, I've been plotting my own way for a while, and now I'm stuck. However long I'm here and wherever I'm headed next, I choose to trust in You. Amen.*

# The Pits

*So when Joseph came to his brothers, they stripped him
of his robe, the robe of many colors that he wore.
And they took him and threw him into a pit.*
GENESIS 37:23–24

**P**ut yourself in Joseph's place, down in that pit. How would
you respond? Would you shout in anger? Would you stare
at the sky, waiting, hoping it was all a joke? Would you frantically search for a foothold, trying to climb up and out? Would
you slump in a heap and cry? Would you think, *Hey, God must
be using this experience to shape me. If I'll just hang in here,
something wonderful will unfold!*

The Bible is silent on Joseph's time in the pit. We don't know
if he fidgeted or fretted or fumed. Maybe he prayed. But we can
see the results of what must have been a confusing and hurtful
experience. As in the lives of Sarah, Ruth, David, Mary, and so
many others, we know where each rocky path led and how God
was at work every step of the way.

You see, the pit was just the beginning. In the years that
followed, Joseph met with good and bad, sometimes *very* bad.
He became a slave, proved his worth in Potiphar's household,
then was falsely accused and imprisoned. He interpreted dreams,
managed long-term famine, and ultimately forgave. Somewhere
along the rocky path, Joseph understood that God was molding
him into the man he needed to be. God was directing the events

of his life for greater good. As he reunited with the very brothers who had thrown him into the pit, he said, "Do not fear, for am I in the place of God? As for you, you meant evil against me, but God meant it for good, to bring it about that many people should be kept alive, as they are today" (Genesis 50:19–20).

Looking back, you see God's hand in your life. Through the good and bad, and sometimes very bad, you can pinpoint where you were headed and how God was shaping you each moment. The trouble is seeing while you're in the middle of life, in the pit. With the walls towering around you, the sky only a patch overhead, how can you imagine something better *beyond*? It takes faith. "Now faith is the assurance of things hoped for, the conviction of things not seen" (Hebrews 11:1). Have faith that God is present. Have faith that He is at work, even when you can't see Him moving. He has shown Himself faithful over the centuries and won't change now.

*God, even in the pit I will have faith. Please hold my faith steady when it wavers. Keep my eyes focused on You until I can see. Amen.*

# Do What?

*"Be still, and know that I am God. I will be exalted among the nations, I will be exalted in the earth!"*
PSALM 46:10

ook through some advice books and you likely won't find many that instruct, "Stop. Do nothing." There are steps to take, changes to implement, things to *do*. Surely we must foresee, plan, act, tweak. . .get our hands dirty as we grapple with and guide our lives. If we had to walk this earth under our own steam, that mind-set would be logical. Who else will take charge if not us? But as Christians, we don't lead our lives alone.

Of the many lessons in the Bible, a big one is recognizing that no matter how well we're handling things—no matter how much we think, *I've got this!*—our control is under God's control. For some, that idea might be irksome (*What about free will?*). But for those of us who realize, even for brief moments, that we don't have it all together, it's sweet relief. Whether life seems manageable or out of hand, God is still God—and He's got this.

God is in control even through the worst threats of the earth and the nations. As Psalm 46 attests, "Though the earth gives way, though the mountains be moved into the heart of the sea" and while "the nations rage" (verses 2, 6), God is present. In and around the descriptions of disaster, God is at work: "God is our refuge and strength, a very present help in trouble" (verse 1); "God is in the midst of [Jerusalem]; she shall not be moved;

God will help her when morning dawns" (verse 5); "Come, behold the works of the LORD. . . . He makes wars cease to the end of the earth; he breaks the bow and shatters the spear; he burns the chariots with fire" (verses 8–9). And at the end of the psalm we hear His words ringing clear: "Be still, and know that I am God" (verse 10).

All the *doing* is God's. Our part is to stop, to be still, to rest in Him. The New American Standard Bible phrases verse 10 this way: "Cease striving and know that I am God," or the footnoted translation: "Let go. . .and know that I am God." It's okay to take our hands off this life and leave it to God's control. Know that the One who "utters his voice, [and] the earth melts" (verse 6) is God. He is mighty to act. And He is at work in the lives of believers.

*Lord, I grasp for what little control is within reach.*
*But You are always in control. Teach me to be*
*still and know that You are God. Amen.*

# First and Foremost

*The saying is trustworthy and deserving of full acceptance,*
*that Christ Jesus came into the world to save sinners,*
*of whom I am the foremost. But I received mercy for*
*this reason, that in me, as the foremost, Jesus Christ*
*might display his perfect patience as an example*
*to those who were to believe in him for eternal life.*

1 Timothy 1:15–16

You've heard of the apostle Paul? The guy who persecuted Christians and then went on to write large chunks of the New Testament? Considering his early life, he would be the worst candidate for the Lord's work, yet he was exactly the man God wanted for the job. Why? Because God is out to save sinners—the foremost and the least.

From the very beginning, when Eve then Adam helped themselves to the forbidden fruit, we humans have been following our desires instead of God's commands. Consequently, we've been ousted from the garden, parted from our close relationship with God. But through Jesus, God made a way back to the garden, back to a restored relationship with Him. And His love is so immense, His sacrifice so perfect, that all of us can find redemption at the cross: "For 'everyone who calls on the name of the Lord will be saved' " (Romans 10:13).

So as Paul (called Saul before his conversion) was headed to Damascus, "still breathing threats and murder against the disciples of the Lord" (Acts 9:1), the Lord met him on the road and transformed him inside and out. Despite Paul's sin, God had plans for his life. As the Lord told Ananias, "[Saul] is a chosen instrument of mine to carry my name before the Gentiles and kings and the children of Israel" (Acts 9:15). With Paul as an example, God demonstrated just how powerful He is to save.

Maybe you believe there's no way you can be an example to others. If that's the case, think about these words of Paul: "For consider your calling, brothers: not many of you were wise according to worldly standards, not many were powerful, not many were of noble birth. But God chose what is foolish in the world to shame the wise; God chose what is weak in the world to shame the strong; God chose what is low and despised in the world, even things that are not, to bring to nothing things that are" (1 Corinthians 1:26–28). God called you, He redeemed you, and now He chooses to use you—whoever you are—for His glory.

*Lord, You are patient and merciful toward even the worst of sinners. May my life, like Paul's, be proof that You save. Amen.*

# Uphill

"May the LORD our God be with us, as He was with our
fathers. May He not leave us nor forsake us, that He may
incline our hearts to Himself, to walk in all His ways,
and to keep His commandments and His statutes and
His judgments, which He commanded our fathers."
1 KINGS 8:57–58 NKJV

E yes focusing straight ahead, fingers gripping the handle-
bars, legs pumping the pedals around and around—she's
determined to reach the summit. Losing steam, growing weary,
she's almost there. . .the top, the relief—and now the reward.
Wind cooling her hot face, muscles relaxed, legs outstretched as
the bike glides down the other side of the hill. If only the ascent
were as sweet as this!

Does your faith walk resemble the uphill push more often
than not? You strain to follow God—to walk in His ways, to
keep His commandments—only to come up short. Your flesh is
always present, pulling you down even as you seek to go up.
You recognize yourself all too clearly in Paul's words: "For I do
not understand my own actions. For I do not do what I want,
but I do the very thing I hate" (Romans 7:15). The reality is no
matter how much we pressure ourselves to live uprightly, we
won't succeed. Paul wrote of himself what is true for all believers: "Nothing good dwells in me, that is, in my flesh. For I have
the desire to do what is right, *but not the ability to carry it out*"

(Romans 7:18, emphasis added). We can't obey God on our own. We lack the ability.

Before you're tempted to ditch the bike and camp out on the side of the hill, consider this: the desire to follow, "to do what is right," is itself from God. He is already at work. When King Solomon, the wisest man ever to live, blessed Israel, he asked that God would be with His people and "incline [their] hearts to Himself." Only then would the Israelites "walk in all His ways." We *can* triumph over the flesh, but we need to rely on God—first for leading us to follow, then for empowering us to follow through. Our outward following and victory result from His leading and power within.

Whatever uphill battles we face, let's not start pedaling without going to God. The One who draws our hearts close to Himself will be by our side giving us the extra boost we need to reach the summit and sweet reward.

*God, I try and try to do the right things, but so often*
*I feel like I'm pedaling uphill. I know You're calling me*
*to walk in Your ways—please help me obey. Amen.*

# Potter and Clay

*But now, O Lord, you are our Father; we are the clay,*
*and you are our potter; we are all the work of your hand.*
ISAIAH 64:8

I f you've ever watched a potter at a potter's wheel, you know that the process of transforming a lump of clay into a vessel takes time. The potter's skilled hands coax the clay up and then press it down, up and down, softening and molding and smoothing it into the intended shape. Sometimes the potter seems to undo work already done, but each movement builds on the previous one until the vessel is complete.

Just so, our heavenly Father is the Master Potter, and our lives are clay in His hands. We are "the work of [His] hand," as Isaiah says. Over time God forms our lives, working them into vessels for His glory. He is even powerful enough to take a "ruined" pot and re-form it. In Jeremiah we read:

> This is the word the Lord spoke to Jeremiah:
> "Go down to the potter's house, and I will
> give you my message there." So I went down
> to the potter's house and saw him working
> at the potter's wheel. He was using his hands
> to make a pot from clay, but something went
> wrong with it. So he used that clay to make
> another pot the way he wanted it to be.

*Then the L*ORD* spoke his word to me:*
*"Family of Israel, can't I do the same thing*
*with you?" says the L*ORD*. "You are in my*
*hands like the clay in the potter's hands."*
(Jeremiah 18:1–6 NCV)

Israel had abandoned God's ways, and as a result God warned that judgment was coming. Yet if Israel repented, God would halt judgment and instead reshape the nation, restoring Israel to His favor. Like the Israelites, our lives can become misshapen and marred because of sin. Hope is not lost, though. In His mercy, God offers us the chance to repent and be reshaped just as He wants us to be.

Alone, we would never produce the beautiful vessel God has in mind. We can't. We aren't the potter. But as clay in the Potter's hand, our lives become new. As we yield to Him, He daily fashions us into His daughters. Even when the pot looks like a lump on the wheel, we never need to doubt the Potter's skill. He envisions the end before He begins. He softens, molds, and smooths with precision, and He won't leave the pot unfinished.

*Father, forgive me when I wander from Your ways.*
*I hear You calling. Please draw me back to*
*You as clay ready to be shaped. Amen.*

# Where God Leads

*But Ruth said, "Do not urge me to leave you or to return from following you. For where you go I will go, and where you lodge I will lodge. Your people shall be my people, and your God my God."*

RUTH 1:16

❧

R uth was one radical woman. After her husband died and her widowed mother-in-law, Naomi, made plans to return to Bethlehem, Ruth could have gone back to her hometown. She could have gone back to familiar faces and gods. She could have gone back to a more thriving marriage pool. But she didn't.

Why? No one would have blamed Ruth for leaving Naomi. It was the sensible thing to do, after all. Naomi even encouraged Ruth to accompany her sister-in-law on the trip back to Moab. Yet Ruth remained firm. She chose following Naomi and her God over all else. She chose faithfulness to others and faith that God would be faithful in return. Ultimately, Ruth stood out for her commitment, so much so that when Ruth met Boaz, her future husband, Boaz said to her, "All that you have done for your mother-in-law since the death of your husband has been fully told to me, and how you left your father and mother and your native land and came to a people that you did not know before. The LORD repay you for what you have done, and a full reward be given you by the LORD, the God of Israel, under whose wings you have come to take refuge!" (Ruth 2:11–12). God *did* reward

Ruth, first with provisions and safety, then with marriage and a son. But God had bigger plans still. Beyond earthly blessings, Ruth's willingness to follow led her to the privilege of becoming a lasting part of God's kingdom work. Ruth and Boaz were the great-grandparents of King David, in the lineage of Jesus Christ.

At the outset Ruth didn't know where following would lead. Even at the end of her life, she likely didn't know how God would use her faithfulness to bless countless others. She had to take each day one after the other, trusting God to take care of the rest. Are we willing to throw ourselves under the protection of God's wings and entrust what's to come to Him? Wherever He has us today, and wherever He might lead us tomorrow, one thing is certain: He is present and active. And He can do great things with our willingness to stick close to Him.

*Lord, my life feels a little like Ruth's. I don't know what will happen as I take these next steps in faith, but I trust You to do wonderful things through me. Amen.*

# With His Help

*And next to him was Shallum the son of Hallohesh,*
*leader of half the district of Jerusalem;*
*he and his daughters made repairs.*

NEHEMIAH 3:12 NKJV

It was a monumental task. Jerusalem's walls were heaps of rubble. And here came Nehemiah, rallying the Jews to rebuild. Work began, but so did the taunts: "When Sanballat heard [that the Jews] were rebuilding the wall, he was very angry, even furious. He made fun of the Jewish people. He said to his friends and those with power in Samaria, 'What are these weak Jews doing? . . . Can they bring stones back to life from piles of trash and ashes?' Tobiah the Ammonite, who was next to Sanballat, said, 'If a fox climbed up on the stone wall they are building, it would break it down' " (Nehemiah 4:1–3 NCV). How did Nehemiah respond to such mockery? He prayed. But even though the work continued, Jerusalem's enemies only upped the hostility. Opposition soon forced the people to work with one hand and hold a weapon with the other (Nehemiah 4:17). In short, the task was crazy. It was bold. It could only happen if God worked through His people.

Faith in their God brought together Jews from all walks of life and kept them going despite mounting trouble. And at the completion of the project (in a mere fifty-two days), no one could doubt who was behind the success. Nehemiah recounted,

"When all our enemies heard of it, all the nations around us were afraid and fell greatly in their own esteem, for they perceived that this work had been accomplished with the help of our God" (Nehemiah 6:16). Without God, the mockers would have had the last word. Without God, the walls would have remained rubble.

Church families today sometimes undertake what seem like monumental tasks. We send missionaries to areas firmly resistant to the Gospel. We raise large amounts of money to plant churches. We minister to communities facing unimaginable crisis. Whatever the task, one mind-set is paramount: the work happens as God works through His people. Without God, ears are deaf to the Good News, funds run out, needs go unmet. But with God. . .we can do the impossible (Matthew 17:20).

What monumental task is before you and your church today? Begin by asking God to work through you. God is just as mighty as He was in Nehemiah's day, and as we join together with fellow believers, He works through us to achieve even the impossible.

*God, You know what we are setting out to do.*
*Be with us. Work through us. May we accomplish*
*big things in Your name. Amen.*

# Press On!

*Not that I have already obtained this or am already perfect. . . .*
*But one thing I do: forgetting what lies behind and straining*
*forward to what lies ahead, I press on toward the goal for*
*the prize of the upward call of God in Christ Jesus.*
PHILIPPIANS 3:12–14

Maybe you're familiar with this frightening feeling. You pull into your garage after a long day at work and realize you don't really remember the drive home. You're so used to the route that your brain went on autopilot, and voilà, here you are. Equally as dangerous is becoming so consumed by what's in your rearview mirror (like the vehicle glued to your bumper) that you stop looking forward.

Rearview driving can be disastrous.

Rearview living can be detrimental too. According to Philippians, when it comes to the Christian life, the best advice is to forget what's behind us and focus on what's ahead. But what are we to forget and what are we to focus on. . .and why?

"Forgetting what lies behind" applies both to past sins that can weigh us down with guilt and to past good works that can puff us up with pride. Letting go of these former failures and successes allows us to take hold of what God has planned next. After all, the first thing God does in a Christian's life is exchange old for new. "The old things have gone; everything is made new!" says 2 Corinthians 5:17 (NCV). And God continues transforming us for good (Philippians 1:6). Our energy goes toward becoming more like Christ in this moment and in a glorious future in heaven. Day in, day out, we turn our eyes to God and focus on Him. We tune our hearts to His Spirit so we can follow His ways. We open our lives to what God is fulfilling through us.

What is He doing in you today? Where can you shift your attention from the rearview mirror and instead look forward and press on? If forgetting the past and pursuing Christlikeness seems too daunting, remember: ultimately God is our means, and He is our reason. It is Christ's work on the cross that redeems us fully. It is Christ's work in us that produces righteousness. Paul wrote, "I press on to make it my own, because Christ Jesus has made me his own" (Philippians 3:12). We owe our present and future to Christ, and through Him we can live lives unburdened by the past.

*Lord, my mind is stuck in the past. Remind me that You are always greater than my sin, that You are the source of my success. Help me press on. Amen.*

# Right on Time

*But do not overlook this one fact, beloved, that with the Lord one day is as a thousand years, and a thousand years as one day. The Lord is not slow to fulfill his promise as some count slowness, but is patient toward you, not wishing that any should perish, but that all should reach repentance.*

2 Peter 3:8–9

~

Late. Late payments are bad. Late starts are frustrating. Most people hate running late (except for being fashionably late to a party). Something that's a long time coming is better late than never. But sometimes it's too little, too late. Even the Rabbit from *Alice in Wonderland* is frantic: "I'm late! I'm late! For a very important date! No time to say hello, goodbye! I'm late! I'm late! I'm late!" Is *late* ever good, really?

When we think about God's promises, it's tempting to shout toward heaven, "You're late!"—particularly when we think about Christ's second coming. It's tempting to believe the scoffers whom Peter wrote about: "They will say, 'Where is the promise of his coming? For ever since the fathers fell asleep, all things are continuing as they were from the beginning of creation' " (2 Peter 3:4). But, as Peter urged, it's important to keep God's promises in perspective. God is so immense that even what seem like the longest spans of time to us are mere blips to Him. Eons are moments. Eternity is a speck within His hands.

Reflect on this: It took a long time to get from the Fall to

Jesus. For generations God's people waited for the promised Messiah. Wouldn't it have been better for God to speed things up? Why wait? Yet in all that time, God was not idle. He was shaping history with precision. Every event that transpired, each person who lived, led to the fulfillment of His perfect plan. Jesus said before His baptism, "God's work, putting things right all these centuries, is coming together right now" (Matthew 3:15 MSG).

God today is the same God as then. In all these years, He has not been idle. He is shaping our days with precision. And what He has promised He will bring about. Meanwhile, this waiting period has purpose. God is not late, but patient. He gives His children time to come to Him. Let's model our heavenly Father and not grow impatient; let's use this time to share what God has done and what He continues to do. Slowly (to us) but surely, God will keep His promise.

*God, Your timing is beyond me. But I'm eternally grateful that You waited long enough for me to turn to You. I pray that many more would do the same. Amen.*

# Prove It

*By this we shall know that we are of the truth and reassure*
*our heart before him; for whenever our heart condemns us,*
*God is greater than our heart, and he knows everything.*
*Beloved, if our heart does not condemn us,*
*we have confidence before God.*
1 John 3:19–21

**A** child beams as she shows off her pristine room, but is the mess just crammed under the bed? An employee types diligently at a computer, but is it Excel or Facebook that holds her attention? A gardener toils for hours, but is her thumb green? The proof is in the pudding. As in, *Mmm, that pudding looks delicious*, but is it? Results equal proof oftentimes. Clothes and toys are in their proper places, so the child cleaned. The spreadsheet is finished on time, so the employee worked. The flowers bloom, so the gardener succeeded. You taste the pudding, and it is indeed good.

Simple examples, but what about something invisible like your salvation? You say you're a Christian. You take God at His word that He saves. Yet how do you know you're saved? Where's the proof in that pudding?

Read through the book of 1 John, and you'll likely catch on to a major theme. Some form of the word *love* appears nearly fifty times in just five short chapters. It's as if John is saying, "In case you missed it, let me repeat it: love, love, love." Because love is fundamental to Christianity. "For God so loved," we're told, that He made a way for sinners to find redemption through His Son (John 3:16). And it is by exhibiting love ourselves that we have proof of God's saving work in us. John wrote, "Beloved, let us love one another, for love is from God, and whoever loves has been born of God and knows God" (1 John 4:7).

On days when you feel less than confident about your salvation, look to your love. Where do you see love manifested? In acts of kindness, big or small. In compassion even for those who hate you. In the pull to reach out to others. . . All flow from a heart that is His. Still unsure? Rest in the words of 1 John: *God is greater.* He is greater than our doubts. He knows our hearts and who belongs to Him. "But God's firm foundation stands, bearing this seal: 'The Lord knows those who are his' " (2 Timothy 2:19).

God saves, and the proof is in our love.

*God, my confidence is a little shaky today. But I believe in Jesus and how He saves me. Remind me, please, of all the ways my life reflects Your love. Amen.*

# What Do You Want?

*He has told you, O man, what is good; and what does*
*the LORD require of you but to do justice, and to love*
*kindness, and to walk humbly with your God?*
MICAH 6:8

ourt is now in session. Micah 6 opens with the Lord's in-
dictment of the people. He pleads His case, how He has
been faithful through the years (verses 3–5). Yet despite His
faithfulness, the people continued to walk their own way. Worse,
their outward attempts at religion (even exaggerated ones) did
nothing to change their insides. Micah rhetorically asked, "With
what shall I come before the LORD, and bow myself before God
on high? . . . Will the LORD be pleased with thousands of rams,
with ten thousands of rivers of oil? Shall I give my firstborn for
my transgression, the fruit of my body for the sin of my soul?"
(Micah 6:6–7). Their pious offering of sacrifices was all for show.
And the Lord was not convinced. He desired something deeper.

Back in Old Testament times, God's people strove to please
Him by keeping the Law and offering sacrifices. But at every step,
with every sin and sacrifice, it was clear that human efforts fell
short. We needed God's ultimate sacrifice, His Son, to redeem
us. Today we gladly accept God's grace. Still, how often do the
sacrifices of the Old Testament morph into our efforts to *do*
more for God? We attend Bible studies throughout the week.
We cram in a community project or two. We spend Sundays

juggling nursery duties, small groups, and worship services. If we aren't careful, our Christian lives begin to look like a one-woman band, this arm doing one thing, that knee doing another. . .

*Wait, what's wrong with those things?* you ask. Nothing! In fact, good works are evidence of faith. As James put it: "Faith by itself, if it does not have works, is dead" (James 2:17). And again, "Show me your faith apart from your works, and I will show you my faith by my works" (James 2:18). The problem occurs if the "outer" takes precedence over the "inner"—if all the *doing* is done without first attending to the heart. God is not impressed by our activities alone, any more than He was impressed by Judah's attempts to cover up sinful habits with sacrifices. He wants something deeper: "For I desire steadfast love and not sacrifice" (Hosea 6:6). God has told us what is good, and it all starts with a relationship with Him.

*Lord, lately I've overlooked the one thing You want most from me. Today I recommit to loving You first and foremost, before I do anything else. Amen.*

# Breaking the Cycle

*Those who are God's children do not continue sinning, because the new life from God remains in them. They are not able to go on sinning, because they have become children of God.*

1 John 3:9 NCV

~

*Y*ou've stumbled. You've slipped up. Sinned. In your mind's eye, you sit slumped on the ground. Dusty. Downtrodden. Discouraged. Will you ever get this right?

The concept of sin after salvation seems contradictory. The moment God saves us, the old self is "crucified" (Romans 6:6). We are made new, and with this newness comes a new allegiance. We no longer bow to sin but to God. Yet no matter how long we've been a Christian, we still struggle with sin. Our redeemed self still contends with our humanness—with the flesh and its desires. Paul wrote in Romans, "For I delight in the law of God, in my inner being, but I see in my members another law waging war against the law of my mind and making me captive to the law of sin that dwells in my members" (7:22–23). Our new nature perceives sin differently now. So begins the struggle. As we grow in our knowledge of God's holiness, we feel our sin more and more. Paul's sin was so evident to him that he cried out, "Wretched man that I am! Who will deliver me from this body of death?" (7:24). But just as quickly as Paul asks the question, he supplies the blessed answer: "Thanks be to God through Jesus

Christ our Lord!" (7:25).

God rescues us from the cycle of sin. Although sin is present and we will stumble at times, sin is not the norm. The Holy Spirit is also present, and His presence makes it impossible for us to keep sinning endlessly. Patterns of righteousness replace patterns of sin with glorious results: "Little children, let no one deceive you. Whoever practices righteousness is righteous, as he is righteous. . . . By this it is evident who are the children of God" (1 John 3:7, 10). Christ's nature as God's Son is imparted to His children, allowing us to mirror Christ's righteous ways, however imperfectly.

First John 3:9 (NCV) tells us that we as God's children "are not able to go on sinning." If you find yourself slumped on the ground, take heart! God's grace and the new life He has given us empower us to pick ourselves up, dust ourselves off, and keep trying. Indeed, we *will* keep trying. We cannot do otherwise.

*Lord, on the ground, it's easy to feel stuck in sin.*
*Thank You for the reminder that sin does not*
*define my life. Your righteousness does. Amen.*

## Here and Now

*"For if you keep silent at this time, relief and deliverance will rise for the Jews from another place, but you and your father's house will perish. And who knows whether you have not come to the kingdom for such a time as this?"*

ESTHER 4:14

❧

**P**ut yourself in the book of Esther. Go ahead—immerse yourself. Read each word without anticipating the next sentence. Picture what's happening without rushing ahead to what's next. Take it moment by moment. Did you notice anything?

We have a tremendous gift in the Bible—the ability to see stories of faith played out. But as a result, we usually read about Abraham and Moses and Mary from a bird's-eye view of sorts. We witness the arc of events. We're privy to how the story ends. And through it all we watch God work. Looking at your own life, you might think, *If only things were so clear!* Of course, we don't have a bird's-eye view of our lives. We can't really see beyond this moment.

Neither could Esther. All along—from her arrival at the palace to twelve months of beauty treatments, from meeting the king to becoming queen—Esther, like us, had to live one day at a time. Moment by moment. And when she faced perhaps the biggest challenge of her life, she did not know with certainty whether she was the girl for the job or how it all would end. Yet she bravely sent her reply to Mordecai: "Go, gather all the Jews to be found in Susa, and hold a fast on my behalf. . . . Then I will go to the king, though it is against the law, and if I perish, I perish" (Esther 4:16). Without knowing the outcome, she did her part and then watched for the rest to unfold.

One major question concerning the book of Esther is God's apparent nonpresence. Unlike in other biblical accounts, He isn't a named participant. Yet, as John MacArthur has noted, God is undeniably present: "Esther is the classic illustration of God's providence as He, the unseen power, controls everything for His purpose."* Esther's life, then, reflects our experience. Even with faith, we can't always sense God's hand at work. We're restricted to this moment, without a clear view of what's to come. Still, let's never lose sight of God. He is orchestrating our lives with perfect timing, for all the "such a time" moments.

*Lord, no matter how much I try to glimpse tomorrow, I can't see beyond now. Renew my faith that, in this moment, You have a purpose and a plan. Amen.*

*John MacArthur, *The MacArthur Bible Commentary* (Nashville: Thomas Nelson, 2005), 555.

# Sans Words

*Likewise the Spirit helps us in our weakness. For we do not know what to pray for as we ought, but the Spirit himself intercedes for us with groanings too deep for words.*
ROMANS 8:26

───⌇───

From dawn till dusk, the day had been a struggle. Now with heavy limbs and a heavy heart, she kneels to pray. But despite the flurry of thoughts in her mind, words won't come. A sigh is all that escapes. Have you ever been to that place of silence? You can likely think of many effects of a stop there: frustration, weariness, doubt, helplessness, dismay, numbness. . . Your first thoughts might not be too encouraging. In fact, being on your knees and at a loss for words seems anything but positive. Yet it can be.

The Bible is full of promises about prayer:

- *"Ask, and it will be given to you; seek, and you will find; knock, and it will be opened to you."* (Matthew 7:7)

- *"And this is the confidence that we have toward him, that if we ask anything according to his will he hears us."* (1 John 5:14)

- *"Therefore I tell you, whatever you ask in*

*prayer, believe that you have received it,*
*and it will be yours."* (Mark 11:24)

Reading just a few of these promises, we may see prayer as first an action on our part. We *ask*. We *speak*. Right? Sometimes. Prayer is a beautiful communion between the Father and His children. In His love, He listens to our words; He welcomes our prayers. First Peter 3:12 says, " 'For the eyes of the Lord are on the righteous, and his ears are open to their prayer.' " But it is through God's Spirit that we have assurance to kneel at our heavenly Father's knee: "You received the Spirit of adoption by whom we cry out, 'Abba, Father' " (Romans 8:15 NKJV). And this same Spirit who emboldens us to pray also enables us to pray when we cannot utter a word. He intercedes with the Father on our behalf, and because He and the Father are one, no words are required. "He who searches hearts knows what is the mind of the Spirit," we're told in Romans (8:27). Unspoken prayer reaches the Father's ear through the Spirit. What we leave unsaid the Spirit in us conveys. So when you find yourself in that place of silence, remember that you are not on your own. Sometimes we speak. Sometimes we let Him do the talking as only He can.

*God, I don't know what to say. But You know what's on*
*my heart, and the Holy Spirit knows just how to*
*express it without words. Thank You! Amen.*

# Sure-Footed

*For who is God, but the LORD? And who is a rock, except our God?—the God who equipped me with strength and made my way blameless. He made my feet like the feet of a deer and set me secure on the heights.*
PSALM 18:31–33

It's mind blowing. It's a hold-your-breath, grip-the-edge-of-your-seat kind of experience. It's. . .well, *Nature* and footage of goats traversing cliff faces. But in all seriousness, their ability to maneuver up and down and across nearly vertical spaces is remarkable. Even at dizzying heights, their hooves are secure.

If you've ever been hiking, you know how important firm footing is. Loose pebbles on steep paths or jumbles of exposed roots can make difficult hikes even harder. One misplaced step and your feet slip from under you, or your head precedes your heels down the trail. At times, life can seem just as precarious. One wrong move or unexpected event and you lose your balance; your world turns upside down.

King David certainly knew the meaning of precarious. Just a cursory glance at his psalms reveals a life punctuated by fleeing and hiding, enemies and struggles. With all that uncertainty, David's words could have overflowed with insecurity. But David also knew what it felt like to be secure even when life was not. In Psalm 18, he used the image of a deer, hooves "secure on the heights," to describe the sure-footedness that characterized his walk. You see, through all the precariousness, David knew where to go for ultimate security: to God, his rock. It was God who set David's feet firmly on paths that otherwise would have been his downfall. He wrote earlier in Psalm 18, "The LORD is my rock and my fortress and my deliverer, my God, my rock, in whom I take refuge, my shield, and the horn of my salvation, my stronghold. I call upon the LORD, who is worthy to be praised, and I am saved from my enemies" (verses 2–3).

If the path ahead of you seems precarious, focus instead, as David did, on all the ways that God makes His children secure. Need protection? God is our shield. Overwhelmed? Find refuge in Him. See no way out? He is our deliverer. Think all hope is lost? God is salvation. Feeling unsteady? Stand firm on the solid rock. God, who is like no other, will equip us and steady us, making our feet secure even on the roughest paths.

*God, You are one of a kind, worthy of endless praise. I'm heading up a steep trail right now. With each step, plant my feet firmly on the rock. Amen.*

# Stay Awhile

*But the Lord answered her, "Martha, Martha, you are anxious and troubled about many things, but one thing is necessary. Mary has chosen the good portion, which will not be taken away from her."*

LUKE 10:41–42

Martha had too many plates in the air. The Lord had arrived, and she was busily preparing the meal. Were bread and roasting meat competing for space over the fire? Was her worktable cluttered with half-prepped dishes? Was she frantically dashing from kitchen to table? The Bible doesn't flesh out the scene, but it does say that Martha was focused on serving to the point of distraction (verse 40). Lest we think this short account applies only to our next dinner party, consider how crammed our lives have become—and how often the many details distract us from the one thing that's necessary.

Next to her sister, Mary provides a beautiful example for us of centering our lives on the one thing: Jesus. It's not that what Martha chose was bad. Hospitality is a blessing to others and is encouraged in the Bible (Hebrews 13:2). And Mary more than likely did not neglect her share of the work every minute of every day. But when it mattered, Mary chose to shift all her attention to her Lord. She chose to sit at His feet while the lesser things faded for a time.

Think of someone dear to you: husband, boyfriend, friend,

sibling, parent. . . What if you only spent a few minutes with that person each week? Wouldn't there eventually be a distance in your relationship? You might even begin to feel like strangers. As believers, we have the amazing privilege of a personal relationship with almighty God. God offers us the chance to get to know Him. Hear Jesus' words "Martha, Martha" not as a scold, but as a wish: He longs for us to choose "the good portion"—and for a very good reason. We need it. In order to deepen our relationship with the Lord and grow in our faith, we have to draw near. We have to spend time at His feet—worshipping, listening, soaking up His love.

Paul once wrote, "I think that all things are worth nothing compared with the greatness of knowing Christ Jesus my Lord" (Philippians 3:8 NCV). What "nothings" distract us from getting to know Jesus? Where do we funnel our energy to the exclusion of quiet moments at His feet? We have much to gain from choosing the good portion. And what we gain we'll never lose.

*Lord, I'm distracted. A time of stillness with You is the last thing on my mind. Forgive me. Nothing is of greater value than You. Amen.*

# "I Know You!"

*I praise you, for I am fearfully and wonderfully made.*
*Wonderful are your works; my soul knows it very well.*
PSALM 139:14

ike a turtle knows its shell. Like a bird knows its nest. Like a
goldfish knows its bowl. God knows us like the back of His
hand.

Close your eyes and picture yourself. How clearly can you see
the shape of your face? The contours of your body? Each freckle
on your skin? Years of living mean we know ourselves pretty well.
But as much as we know the waves in our hair or the flecks in our
eyes, God's knowledge goes deeper. The psalmist said of God,
"For you formed my inward parts; you knitted me together in
my mother's womb" (Psalm 139:13). God's knowledge is more
than passive familiarity with how we look. He knows everything
that makes us who we are because He formed us, inside and
out, "fearfully and wonderfully."

"That's great!" you say. "But now what?" How does what
God did in the past apply to our present? Well, God didn't stop
at our physical beings. Before we existed, He put in place His
design for us: "Your eyes saw my unformed substance; in your
book were written, every one of them, the days that were formed
for me, when as yet there was none of them" (Psalm 139:16).
Our heavenly Father has planned our days—from the major ones
to the mundane—as intricately and with as much knowledge of

who we are as when He formed our bodies. Today has purpose.

What about the days that are calendars away? God will know us just as deeply then, and His plans still stand. Jesus told believers, "Even the hairs of your head are all numbered. Fear not" (Luke 12:7). As these lives of ours unfold, we never need to fear. We have the promise of God's good will for us: "I know the plans I have for you, declares the LORD, plans for welfare and not for evil, to give you a future and a hope" (Jeremiah 29:11). Today and tomorrow, rest in the sovereignty and goodness of God. He who formed us and planned our days from the beginning continues to watch over us throughout our earthly lives, right down to the end. "He knows our frame; he remembers that we are dust," we read in Psalm 103:14. God has a perfect plan for eternity too, one He set in motion long ago.

God knows us. Like the back of His nail-pierced hand.

*God, how well You know me! How perfectly You have formed my life! I praise You for the wonderful things You do. Amen.*

## Walking Blind

*And I will lead the blind in a way that they do not know,*
*in paths that they have not known I will guide them. I will turn*
*the darkness before them into light, the rough places*
*into level ground. These are the things I do,*
*and I do not forsake them.*

Isaiah 42:16

She heads down the sidewalk. The curb to her right and the building to her left become her guides, keeping her straight. Her cane skims the pavement—back and forth, back and forth—as she searches for anything in her path. She approaches the intersection and listens for the signal, listens to the hum of engines in the traffic on the street.

If you're not blind yourself, just imagining daily activities like walking in your town or crossing a familiar street may be terrifying. Even more so is the thought of maneuvering in an unknown place. There, the fear is real—you wouldn't know which way to turn; you wouldn't know what to expect. That's the scene painted in Isaiah 42:16—the blind and the unknown road ahead. Only the blind in the verse aren't walking alone. They have God at their side, lighting the way, leveling the path.

God has a long history of leading His people in unknown territory. Take the exodus. God used clouds and fire to lead Israel through the wilderness: "And the LORD went before them by day in a pillar of cloud to lead them along the way, and by night in a pillar of fire to give them light. . . . The pillar of cloud by day and the pillar of fire by night did not depart from before the people" (Exodus 13:21–22). Later in Psalms we read, "[God] led out his people like sheep and guided them in the wilderness like a flock. He led them in safety, so that they were not afraid" (Psalm 78:52–53). Day and night God's guiding presence was near. He kept His people safe. He kept them from fear.

Maybe you're facing a wilderness of your own. You don't know which way to turn; you don't know what to expect. When you envision your future, the vision is blank, blurry at best. Remember the words of Isaiah 42: "These are the things I do, and I do not forsake them." God is present. God is leading. He is actively reversing our fears—lighting the way, leveling the path. So link your arm with His and wait to see where He takes you.

*Lord, not seeing what's ahead has my feet glued in place.
But I know You will be with me each step I take.
Replace my fear with faith. Amen.*

# Those He Loves

*My child, do not reject the LORD's discipline, and don't get angry when he corrects you. The LORD corrects those he loves, just as parents correct the child they delight in.*

PROVERBS 3:11–12 NCV

The seconds crawled. Each minute was excruciating. Never in her young life had she suffered so terribly. There—on a stool, in a corner, staring at the wallpaper—the child was stuck in time-out. But her mother knew one thing: the suffering would make her daughter stronger. The unpleasant discipline would yield beautiful results.

In our Christian lives, God's discipline is a topic we'd rather not think about. Why focus on the negative? We need a renewed perspective on this topic. Eventually discipline has a *positive* effect on our lives. All of us stray from the standards of our heavenly Father at times—standards that protect us and enable us to thrive. Discipline corrects our course; it trains us while we grow as God's daughters. Consider these verses:

> *So hold on through your sufferings, because they are like a father's discipline. God is treating you as children. All children are disciplined by their fathers. . . . It is even more important that we accept discipline from the Father of our spirits so we will have life. Our fathers on*

*earth disciplined us for a short time in the way*
*they thought was best. But God disciplines us*
*to help us, so we can become holy as he is. We*
*do not enjoy being disciplined. It is painful at*
*the time, but later, after we have learned from*
*it, we have peace, because we start living in*
*the right way.* (Hebrews 12:7, 9–11 NCV)

Of greater value still than the way discipline transforms us is what discipline tells us about God. Through it, God displays His boundless love. What loving parent would turn a blind eye to behavior that will hinder or, worse yet, hurt their child? God loves us immensely more, and He will not neglect to guide us—for our good.

Everything God does is aimed at restoration. Ever since the Fall, God has been bringing us back to communion with Him. Even in His discipline—the correction that seems to tear us down—God's goal is to build us up. "Blessed is the man whom you discipline, O LORD," the psalmist said (Psalm 94:12). We have so much to gain as we allow the Lord's discipline to do its work. Let's not reject His blessing.

*Lord, those You love, You correct. From now on, I choose*
*to focus on the love behind the discipline—and on the way*
*You are doing something beautiful in me. Amen.*

# Gifted

*Then Moses said to the people of Israel, "See, the L<small>ORD</small>*
*has called by name Bezalel the son of Uri, son of Hur, of the*
*tribe of Judah; and he has filled him with the Spirit of God,*
*with skill, with intelligence, with knowledge, and with all*
*craftsmanship, to devise artistic designs, to work in gold*
*and silver and bronze, in cutting stones for setting,*
*and in carving wood, for work in every skilled craft."*
E<small>XODUS</small> 35:30–33

Take a look around your church congregation some Sunday, and you might be fascinated by the sea of people. Tall and short. Young and old. No shade of hair or skin or eyes exactly the same. And that's just on the surface. God equips each of His children with unique abilities too. One plays an instrument during worship; another greets visitors with a bubbly personality. One plans crafts for Sunday school; another organizes a food drive. One makes repairs around the building; another uses nursing skills on a mission trip. And on the list goes.

God has been equipping His people uniquely for generations. Like Bezalel. Back in Moses' day, Bezalel was one of two named artisans who were involved in the construction of the tabernacle. Based on the description in Exodus 25–30, the project was no small feat. From the curtains to the altars, from the lampstands to the ark, the tabernacle itself and everything in it required great skill to complete. But God, being God, knew what His people would be up against, and He prepared them ahead of time. God "filled [Bezalel] with the Spirit of God, with skill, with intelligence, with knowledge, and with all craftsmanship"—with everything necessary to do the job—abilities that he likely developed over the course of his life. When it was time to begin, Bezalel was ready.

Behind every individual ability is God. Paul wrote to the church in Corinth, "Now there are varieties of gifts, but the same Spirit; and there are varieties of service, but the same Lord; and there are varieties of activities, but it is the same God who empowers them all in everyone" (1 Corinthians 12:4–6). The God who worked through Bezalel works through us today. Each of us is Spirit filled with unique abilities, prepared in us ahead of time. "For we are his workmanship," we read in Ephesians 2:10, "created in Christ Jesus for good works, which God prepared beforehand, that we should walk in them." How has God gifted you? What has He been preparing you to do?

*God, my experiences, my education, my talents. . .
they're no accident. Through them, You are preparing
me to do Your work. Use my gifts for Your glory. Amen.*

# Impossible!

*He did not weaken in faith when he considered his own body,
which was as good as dead (since he was about a hundred
years old), or when he considered the barrenness of Sarah's
womb. No unbelief made him waver concerning the promise
of God, but he grew strong in his faith as he gave glory
to God, fully convinced that God was able
to do what he had promised.*

ROMANS 4:19–21

**Y**ou sit down to your morning coffee and paper and read these headlines: MAN SURVIVES THREE DAYS IN WHALE'S BELLY; LOCAL FISHERMAN WALKS ON WATER; ENTOMBED MAN RAISED TO LIFE; RED SEA SPLITS IN TWO; SACK LUNCH FEEDS THOUSANDS; BLIND SINCE BIRTH—NOW HE SEES! "Impossible!" you say. In most contexts, you'd be correct. But in the Bible, these are only some of the "impossible" things that occurred. Jonah survived being swallowed by a big fish. Peter walked on water briefly. Jesus brought Lazarus back to life after four days in a tomb. God's people crossed the Red Sea on dry ground. Five thousand people feasted on five loaves of bread and two fish. A little mud plus Jesus' touch equaled sight for a man born blind.

The account of Abraham and Sarah is another example of impossibilities happening. God promised Abraham that he would have a son and that, through Isaac, Abraham would become "the father of many nations" (Romans 4:18). One-hundred-year-old

Abraham and ninety-year-old Sarah were hardly candidates for such a promise. Yet that's exactly what God promised and exactly what He fulfilled. The key was believing that *God* would do the impossible. "God was able to do. . . ," we read in Romans 4:21, and Abraham was "fully convinced" of that fact. Later, in Hebrews 11:11, we read that "by faith Sarah herself *received* power to conceive" (emphasis added). Without God in the picture, there would be no promise, let alone fulfillment. But with God at work, the impossible was indeed possible.

Whenever God leads you into the realm of the "impossible," remember: what would be impossible for us alone isn't with God at our side. The angel said to Mary, "Nothing will be impossible with God" (Luke 1:37). Jesus told a demon-possessed boy's father, "All things are possible for one who believes" (Mark 9:23). And speaking of the most impossible thing, the saving of ourselves, Jesus declared, "With man this is impossible, but with God all things are possible" (Matthew 19:26). The One who makes the promise is faithful (Hebrews 10:23), so let's believe in our hearts, even when our heads say, "Impossible!"

*God, You know what I'm facing, and it's impossible!*
*But only when I face it alone. With You, it's no*
*longer impossible. Amen.*

# What's Wrong?

*Search me, O God, and know my heart: try me,*
*and know my thoughts: and see if there be any wicked*
*way in me, and lead me in the way everlasting.*
PSALM 139:23–24 KJV

While each of us may be guilty of fishing for compliments at one time or another, few of us fish for criticism. We want the spotlight on our good side, not the bad. We generally put our best foot forward; we don't ask someone to identify our missteps. "Show me my faults!" is rarely the cry of our hearts. And it's certainly not something we'd relish from the God of the universe, the One who knows absolutely everything about us. Psalm 139 opens, "O LORD, you have searched me and known me! You know when I sit down and when I rise up; you discern my thoughts from afar. You search out my path and my lying down and are acquainted with all my ways. Even before a word is on my tongue, behold, O LORD, you know it altogether" (verses 1–4). If we ask God to tell us what's wrong, He's not going to miss one word, one action, one thought. Yet asking God to tell him what's wrong is precisely what David does. The psalm he begins by declaring God's omniscience, he ends by inviting God to reveal his faults. Why? Because David knew that hiding from God was futile, and that God would reward a humble heart.

On the flip side, those with hearts closed to His instruction will find no place at His table. Jesus told the Pharisees, the religious elite who held tight to self-righteousness, "Those who are well have no need of a physician, but those who are sick. I came not to call the righteous, but sinners" (Mark 2:17). When we seek the Great Physician's care, asking Him to examine us, He will poke and prod and point out where sin still festers inside. It takes humility, and some guts, to open ourselves to God, to face the unpleasantness of our faults. James wrote, "Submit yourselves therefore to God. . . . Cleanse your hands, you sinners, and purify your hearts, you double-minded. Be wretched and mourn and weep. Let your laughter be turned to mourning and your joy to gloom" (James 4:7–9). Ugh. But don't overlook the results. "Humble yourselves before the Lord," James continued, "and he will exalt you" (verse 10).

When we approach the God of the universe and say, "Show me my faults!" He will show us favor (Proverbs 3:34).

*Search me, God. Show me where I am wrong—*
*and where You can make me right. Amen.*

# Portrait of a Woman

*Who can find a virtuous woman?*
*for her price is far above rubies.*
PROVERBS 31:10 KJV

**P**roverbs 31:10 is the first verse of a poem written about a wife and mother. This model of womanhood might intimidate you or irritate you, but God can use these verses to shape us. If you've never read them (or haven't in a while), time to refresh your memory!

> *Who can find a virtuous woman? for her price is far above rubies. The heart of her husband doth safely trust in her, so that he shall have no need of spoil. She will do him good and not evil all the days of her life. She seeketh wool, and flax, and worketh willingly with her hands. She is like the merchants' ships; she bringeth her food from afar. She riseth also while it is yet night, and giveth meat to her household, and a portion to her maidens. She considereth a field, and buyeth it: with the fruit of her hands she planteth a vineyard. She girdeth her loins with strength, and strengtheneth her arms. She perceiveth that her merchandise is good: her candle goeth not out by night. . . . She stretcheth out her hand to the poor; yea, she reacheth*

*forth her hands to the needy. She is not afraid of the snow for her household: for all her household are clothed with scarlet. . . . She maketh fine linen, and selleth it; and delivereth girdles unto the merchant. Strength and honour are her clothing; and she shall rejoice in time to come. She openeth her mouth with wisdom; and in her tongue is the law of kindness. She looketh well to the ways of her household, and eateth not the bread of idleness. Her children arise up, and call her blessed; her husband also, and he praiseth her. . . . Favour is deceitful, and beauty is vain: but a woman that feareth the LORD, she shall be praised.* (Proverbs 31:10–18, 20–21, 24 –28, 30 KJV)

What describes the Proverbs 31 woman? Words like *dependable*, *savvy*, *diligent*, *strong*, *openhanded*, *fearless*, *joyous*, and *caring*. Her crowning glory? Reverence for God. She is a woman of faith, which brings her praise. If you look, you can see aspects of her reflected back at you in the mirror. And as you seek God each day, you'll see her more and more.

*God, please work in me so that I have the heart of a virtuous woman. Amen.*

# The Root of Worry

*"And which of you by being anxious can
add a single hour to his span of life?"*
MATTHEW 6:27

～

The rent is due, but your bank account is empty. You're waiting for the doctor's call. Your car breaks down miles from home. You've sent out dozens of résumés and still don't have a job. Your child is heading off to college. You watch footage of yet another disaster. . . Add worry to any of these situations and what do you get? Headaches, lost sleep, a frazzled mind, sapped joy. . .more worry. Worry just doesn't work. In the moment, worry feels constructive, but it's useless to bring about the positive outcome we hope for. Being anxious won't pay the rent or make the phone ring. Being anxious won't fix a flat or land you a job. Being anxious won't safeguard your child or save the world. As our Lord put it, "Which of you by being anxious can add a single hour to his span of life?"

Bottom line: worry is powerless—but our God is powerful. Near the beginning of His earthly ministry, Jesus called His twelve apostles, and as part of their marching orders, He warned them that they would encounter persecution. "I am sending you out as sheep in the midst of wolves," He said (Matthew 10:16). If ever words could cause anxiety, those words could. But Jesus also told the apostles not to worry: "And do not fear those who kill the body but cannot kill the soul. . . . Are not two sparrows sold for a penny? And not one of them will fall to the ground apart from your Father. But even the hairs of your head are all numbered. Fear not, therefore; you are of more value than many sparrows" (Matthew 10:28–31). God controlled everything, even down to a tiny sparrow's death; He would certainly watch over His own.

When worry grips our lives, it's a sure sign of misplaced focus. We focus too much on ourselves and not enough on God. We forget all God can do for us and in us. Paul preceded his oft-quoted verse on worry—"Do not be anxious about anything, but in everything by prayer and supplication with thanksgiving let your requests be made known to God" (Philippians 4:6)—with five crucial words: "The Lord is at hand" (4:5). Because God is near, we do not need to be anxious. Because God is in control, we do not need to fear.

*Lord, I confess, I'm a worrywart. Forgive me. Forgive me for trying to take control of what only You can control. I leave my anxiety with You. Amen.*

# Lights On!

*"You are the light of the world. A city set on a hill cannot be hidden. Nor do people light a lamp and put it under a basket, but on a stand, and it gives light to all in the house. In the same way, let your light shine before others, so that they may see your good works and give glory to your Father who is in heaven."*
MATTHEW 5:14–16

A child wakes up in the night. Shadows lurk around the room. Shapes loom in the darkness. But with the glow of a night-light, the shadows disperse, and the shapes transform into her sturdy dresser, her plush chair. A woman sits in a dark campsite. Every sound is amplified. It's as if a murky curtain surrounds her, blocking her sight. But with the light of a fire, she sees the canopy of majestic trees, branches rustling in the wind. Introduce light into darkness and everything changes.

Before we knew Christ, we lived in spiritual darkness. We were blinded by sin and unable to see our way out. But God, "the Father of lights" (James 1:17), did not leave us in the dark. He called us, and He offered His light. In one of his letters to the Corinthians, Paul wrote, "For God, who said, 'Let light shine out of darkness,' has shone in our hearts to give the light of the knowledge of the glory of God in the face of Jesus Christ" (2 Corinthians 4:6). When God's light enters our hearts, when spiritual truth once veiled becomes visible, everything changes.

God works a total transformation in us. Sinful to righteous. Old to new. Dark to light. "For at one time you were darkness, but now you are light in the Lord" (Ephesians 5:8).

Our role? "Walk as children of light (for the fruit of light is found in all that is good and right and true)" (Ephesians 5:8–9). God's enlightening produces fruit in us, and as our transformed lives reflect the good and the right and the true, others are drawn like moths. God uses our light to shed light, to "proclaim the excellencies of him who called [us] out of darkness into his marvelous light" (1 Peter 2:9).

Our world is a dark one, and the darkness often causes us to shrink back. Hiding our light—fitting in instead of standing out—is easy to do. But Jesus called believers "the light of the world," and then He told us to let the light shine. He held nothing back to bring us light. Let's shine for Him!

*Lord, I want to be light in darkness,*
*so bright that no one misses You. Amen.*

# Cradle to Grave

*"Listen to me, O house of Jacob, all the remnant of the house of Israel, who have been borne by me from before your birth, carried from the womb; even to your old age I am he, and to gray hairs I will carry you. I have made, and I will bear; I will carry and will save."*

ISAIAH 46:3–4

We begin getting older from the moment we are born. Up to a certain age, aging is a reason to celebrate. Babies receive joyous applause as they learn to crawl then walk. Children look forward to each birthday party. Teenagers count down the days till sweet sixteen. College students can't wait to head off to school and freedom! . . . But at what age does aging lose its luster? When our twenties (or thirties, or forties. . .) are past tense? When we spot that first gray hair? When our batteries run down faster than they charge up? When the kids we used to babysit have kids? When we're *ma'am*, not *miss*, to almost everybody? When our high school photos look dated? When we realize we're getting *older* and there's nothing we can do about it?

While there's nothing we can do to keep ourselves from aging—nothing we can do to stop the dates on the calendar from coming and going—there's still good news. God's care has no expiration date. As the Lord promised to Israel in Isaiah 46, He is the same God year in, year out. Just as He cared in the past, He will continue to care.

The psalmist who wrote Psalm 71 knew what it meant to rely on God's faithfulness even when confronted with this ugly kicker: passing time doesn't exempt us from troubles. Despite being older, the psalmist had enemies to deal with, enemies who sought his life (verse 10). Yet he remained confident of God's care. He knew God would stand by him no matter how old he was: "Even to old age and gray hairs, O God, do not forsake me. . . . Your righteousness, O God, reaches the high heavens. You who have done great things, O God, who is like you? You who have made me see many troubles and calamities will revive me again; from the depths of the earth you will bring me up again. You will increase my greatness and comfort me again" (verses 18–21).

No matter your age, cling to God's promise: He will revive and comfort. He will carry and save.

*God, sometimes the thought of aging is overwhelming.
So I'll think of Your promises instead. Amen.*

# Lives That Talk

*Many Samaritans from that town believed in him because of the woman's testimony, "He told me all that I ever did."*

John 4:39

**G**od could never use me! Has that thought ever crossed your mind? *My past is too complicated. My present is too frayed. My act just isn't together.* If asked if God could use her, the Samaritan woman in John's Gospel might have felt the same. She was an outcast with a past. Would she ever have guessed that God would handpick her for a special role in His kingdom work? That is, in fact, exactly what He did.

We're introduced to the Samaritan woman on a journey from Judea. Jesus and His disciples were on their way to Galilee, and Jesus, tired from all the walking, sat down at a well. A woman showed up toting her water jar, but the meeting was no accident. John's statement that Jesus "had to pass through Samaria" (John 4:4) implies intention. Our Lord chose the road through Samaria with a purpose, and it wasn't to save time, although that particular route was a well-established shortcut. He was on a mission from His Father that included this lone Samaritan woman. As with all that God does, the timing was perfect. When the woman arrived, Jesus was waiting. Immediately, He bucked expectations by asking for some water. Here was a Samaritan woman with a bad reputation, and Jesus—a Jewish religious leader—speaks with her. No cultural barrier and nothing from her past would prevent

Him from reaching out. Then, over the course of the conversation, He would confront the woman with her sin, discuss theological truth, offer living water, and reveal Himself as Messiah. Far from dismissing her, Jesus was calling her to Himself. The disciples, returning just in time to hear Jesus' declaration of who He was, "marveled" at what they witnessed (John 4:27). But God was not amazed or surprised. It was all part of His plan.

The one who was an outcast God wanted to use to spread His message. He took the ragged bits and began making them whole, and in response, the woman abandoned her water jar and rushed to town to boldly share her experience with those who, until then, had rejected her. So powerful was God's work in her that her testimony caused a domino effect as "many more" sought Jesus and believed (John 4:41).

God was only getting started using the Samaritan woman's life to inspire others. He's still using it some two thousand years later.

*God, can You use me? My life seems like such a mess.*
*But I forget that Your work within me is what*
*makes my messy life beautiful. Amen.*

# Great Expectations

*Now unto him that is able to do exceeding abundantly
above all that we ask or think, according to
the power that worketh in us.*

<small>EPHESIANS 3:20 KJV</small>

**A**re you an expecter? Expecting things comes naturally. When you go on vacation, you expect to have a good time. When you purchase something, you expect to get what you pay for. When your kids are running late, you expect them to let you know. When your friend wants to stop by for a visit, you expect her to call first. When your brother makes a promise, you expect him to follow through. Life is full of expectations. In fact, while whatever else we bring to a given situation may vary, we usually come with expectations—of what's going to happen, of how we're going to feel, of what someone else is going to do. . . We're glad when our expectations are met, but how do we respond when they're not? And what about our expectations of God?

Too often we have low expectations of God, and the fault stems from our humanity. We tend to frame what's possible using our human lens. What we pray for, what we expect to happen, is limited if we aren't viewing the situation from the perspective of our limitless God. God isn't just able to meet our expectations. He isn't just able to exceed them either. Ephesians 3:20 says He is able to do "exceeding abundantly" more. So how do we claim this truth for ourselves? To understand the how, backtrack a handful of verses to the beginning of Paul's prayer:

> *For this cause I bow my knees unto the Father of our Lord Jesus Christ, of whom the whole family in heaven and earth is named, that he would grant you, according to the riches of his glory, to be strengthened with might by his Spirit in the inner man; that Christ may dwell in your hearts by faith; that ye, being rooted and grounded in love, may be able to comprehend with all saints what is the breadth, and length, and depth, and height; and to know the love of Christ, which passeth knowledge, that ye might be filled with all the fulness of God.* (Ephesians 3:14–19 KJV)

It all comes back to "the power that worketh *in us*." If we are to know "exceeding abundantly" firsthand, self has to step aside and let God work. It's the Holy Spirit strengthening. It's Christ indwelling. It's God's love rooting. And as we are filled to the brim with God, His power overflows in us—far exceeding our expectations.

*Father, forgive my low expectations. You are able to do exceedingly abundantly more than I could ever imagine. Amen.*

# What's the Plan?

*The heart of man plans his way,*
*but the LORD establishes his steps.*
PROVERBS 16:9

Interviewer: "Where do you see yourself in five years?" Applicant: "In five years. . ." Although we may dread (or mentally roll our eyes at) this cookie-cutter interview question, it's a good one, really. Having plans or goals shows that we're motivated and forward-thinking. It reveals our priorities. Plus, knowing where we're headed helps us get there. But when, as Christians, we plan the next year or decade or beyond, we need to follow one simple rule: Don't leave God out of the equation.

*Don't* leave God out of the equation? Is it possible *to* leave Him out? He is almighty God, after all, the One of whom Isaiah wrote: "The LORD of hosts has sworn: 'As I have planned, so shall it be, and as I have purposed, so shall it stand. . . .' This is the purpose that is purposed concerning the whole earth, and this is the hand that is stretched out over all the nations. For the LORD of hosts has purposed, and who will annul it? His hand is stretched out, and who will turn it back?" (Isaiah 14:24, 26–27). On one level we know God is in all things and controls all things. Yet how often do we act, perhaps unconsciously, as if we can run our lives without Him? Instead, we should take our cue from Jesus. When speaking to the crowd at Capernaum, Jesus said, "For I have come down from heaven, not to do my own will but the will of him who sent me" (John 6:38). Later, when the hour was drawing near for His crucifixion, Jesus prayed, "My Father, if it be possible, let this cup pass from me; nevertheless, not as I will, but as you will" (Matthew 26:39). If Christ, who is one with God, bent His will to the Father's—even in the most bitter of circumstances—how much more should we?

The next time you make plans, keep these instructions in mind: "Come now, you who say, 'Today or tomorrow we will go into such and such a town and spend a year there and trade and make a profit'—yet you do not know what tomorrow will bring. . . . Instead you ought to say, 'If the Lord wills, we will live and do this or that' " (James 4:13–15). Place God first before the plan. Include Him in the process. You'll find that when you partner with God, you succeed (Proverbs 16:3).

*Father, I have so many plans! Today I hand them over to You. May Your will be done, not mine. Amen.*

# Powered by the Spirit

*If we live by the Spirit, let us also keep*
*in step with the Spirit.*
GALATIANS 5:25

We see examples of it every day. Electricity makes a light-bulb burn. Wind makes a kite fly. Water makes a blade of grass green. Fire makes a marshmallow toast. Gasoline makes an engine run. One thing powers another. A similar phenomenon takes place in us as Christians. The Holy Spirit is our fuel—a high-octane fuel.

The Holy Spirit, being one with God, is powerful—so powerful that He raised Christ from the dead (Romans 8:11). As believers, we have access to the Holy Spirit from the moment of salvation when the Holy Spirit enters our beings. Paul explained in Ephesians, "In him you also, when you heard the word of truth, the gospel of your salvation, and believed in him, were sealed with the promised Holy Spirit" (Ephesians 1:13). The outgrowth of the indwelling Spirit is power (Acts 1:8). How much power? A mind-boggling amount. Zechariah's fifth vision is just one of many illustrations in the Bible of the power available to believers through the Spirit. Following the captivity in Babylon, Israel returned home and began rebuilding the temple, but the work stalled. Zechariah's vision functioned as reassurance to Zerubbabel, a civil leader, to keep on with the work because even what wasn't humanly possible was attainable when accomplished by the Spirit. The angel told Zechariah, "This is the word of the LORD to Zerubbabel: Not by might, nor by power, but by my Spirit, says the LORD of hosts. Who are you, O great mountain? Before Zerubbabel you shall become a plain" (Zechariah 4:6–7).

The power that flattened mountains—or rebuilt temples—is our power also to live a godly life. Without the Holy Spirit we are susceptible to sin, all the "works of the flesh" listed in Galatians 5:19–21. But with the Spirit we have supernatural power to over-come and a bounty of good fruit that He produces in our lives: "Walk by the Spirit, and you will not gratify the desires of the flesh. For the desires of the flesh are against the Spirit. . . . But the fruit of the Spirit is love, joy, peace, patience, kindness, good-ness, faithfulness, gentleness, self-control" (Galatians 5:16–17, 22–23). Given these benefits, what stops us from tapping into our fuel source every day? The results are powerful when we spend time in the Word and on our knees, when we walk side by side with the Spirit.

*Holy Spirit, You are my fuel: You counsel me,
You fortify me, You comfort me, You empower
me. . . For all You do, I give thanks. Amen.*

# Looking Ahead

*"Remember not the former things, nor consider the things of old. Behold, I am doing a new thing; now it springs forth, do you not perceive it? I will make a way in the wilderness and rivers in the desert."*

ISAIAH 43:18–19

⁓

**R**emember when. . ." It's the familiar chorus that begins reminiscences. "Remember when we used to spend summers at the lake?" "Remember when we stayed up all night cramming for that exam?" "Remember when Dad got me a puppy for my birthday?" "Remember when we had that lemonade stand?" "Remember when we took those ski lessons?" Remembering old times can bring smiles among friends and family. In terms of our faith, remembering what's come before and what God has done can buoy us in rough waters. So why does the Lord tell His people to "remember not the former things, nor consider the things of old"?

God had a long history of delivering Israel in astonishing ways. Just think of the string of plagues followed by the grand finale of the Red Sea splitting in two that freed the nation from Egyptian rule. But as much as God wanted His people to remember His previous mighty acts, He also wanted them to know that He was not finished delivering them. "Therefore, behold, the days are coming, declares the LORD, when it shall no longer be said, 'As the LORD lives who brought up the people of Israel out of the land of Egypt,' but 'As the LORD lives who brought up the people of Israel out of the north country and out of all the countries where he had driven them' " (Jeremiah 16:14–15). If the Israelites thought God's deliverance from Egypt was something, it was nothing compared to God's deliverance from Babylon. And still-greater things were yet on the horizon. When the Lord says, "Remember not the former things," it is because He is "doing a new thing"—ushering in Messiah and drawing Israel ever closer to ultimate restoration.

Looking back over your life, where have you seen God work mightily on your behalf? Where can you say, "Remember when God. . ."? Memories of God's faithfulness are beautiful blessings. Gain confidence from all God has done. Allow His track record to build up your faith. *But* don't stop looking forward. Keep your eyes trained on how God is working in you today. . .and tomorrow. Anticipate the "new thing" He is doing, because greater things are yet to come.

*God, when I survey the life I've lived so far, I can see Your fingerprints all over it. Reveal to me all the new things You are doing too. Amen.*

# A Piece of Advice

*Keep me from looking at worthless things.*
*Let me live by your word.*
PSALM 119:37 NCV

You can find advice around every corner, it seems. From billboards to magazines to the internet to your aunt Louise, there's no shortage of sources if you want to learn the "secret" of living well. Want to be happier? There's a top-ten list of tips to try. Want to reboot your mind, body, or spirit? There's an array of diet plans to follow. Want to succeed? There's a successful person's book that will tell you how. Want to breathe better? Yes, there's a book on that too. While much of this advice can be helpful, it shouldn't be the Christian's first resort. If we want to find life—thriving, abundant life—we need to go to the source.

God is our source of life, and He has given us His Word as the source of wisdom on living well. Shortly before Moses' death and before the people entered Canaan, Moses reminded Israel of all God had told him throughout the years in the wilderness. Some of his final advice was "Take to heart all the words I have solemnly declared to you this day, so that you may command your children to obey carefully all the words of this law. *They are not just idle words for you—they are your life.* By them you will live long in the land you are crossing the Jordan to possess" (Deuteronomy 32:46–47 NIV, emphasis added). God's words to His people were not hollow; they were essential to living the life of fullness God desired for them. The nation was to cling to God's law as if its life depended on it, which, of course, it did.

Believers today receive life—that is, eternal life to come in heaven—through believing in the Word, Jesus Christ, and they also receive life—spiritual nourishment and growth—through ingesting God's Word, the Bible. When the devil tempted Jesus, he first used Jesus' hunger. After forty days and nights without eating, Jesus was hungry (Matthew 4:2), but He had a means of subsistence that was even more valuable than physical food. He said, "It is written, 'Man shall not live by bread alone, but by every word that comes from the mouth of God' " (Matthew 4:4). God's Word is a powerful resource in our lives. Now, just as in the psalmist's day, our prayer should be to have eyes turned from the world and focused on the Word. Our life depends on it.

*Lord, when my life is a jumble of self-improvement, shift my attention back to Your Word. Amen.*

# Running to Win

*Therefore, since we are surrounded by so great a cloud
of witnesses, let us also lay aside every weight, and sin
which clings so closely, and let us run with endurance
the race that is set before us, looking to Jesus,
the founder and perfecter of our faith.*
HEBREWS 12:1–2

The runner took her mark as the crowd of curious spectators watched. Decked in clunky, loosely tied boots, baggy pants, and dangling jewelry, she looked like a running disaster waiting to happen. Either she'd trip on her laces or she'd catch her arm in her necklace. Even if she managed to escape those perils, the excess material of her pants would surely slow her down. She needed to get ready for the race. The author of Hebrews used a race as a metaphor for entering and pursuing the Christian life. Athletes in ancient times would remove any unnecessary garments before competing. With no extra weight and with nothing to trip them, they could run to win. Applying the metaphor to our lives, we too need to get ready for the race.

The Christian "race" is no easy sprint down the track. Our Lord guarantees tribulation (John 16:33), and the apostles' lives certainly reflected that troubles are a fact of the Christian life. Paul wrote the Corinthians, "For we do not want you to be unaware, brothers, of the affliction we experienced in Asia. For we were so utterly burdened beyond our strength that we despaired of life itself" (2 Corinthians 1:8). Each of us knows from our own experience that temptation and trials are inevitable. The Christian race, then, is more of a cross-country, long-distance obstacle course. So how do we prepare?

One way is by drawing inspiration from "the cloud of witnesses" mentioned in Hebrews; the Bible is filled with examples of faithful men and women whose lives pump us up to keep going. Another way we prepare is by ridding our lives of anything that hinders us. What distracts us from the race? What slows us down? What sins do we cling to that will only cause us to stumble? By letting these go, we're running to win. "Do you not know that in a race all the runners run, but only one receives the prize?" Paul wrote. "So run that you may obtain it. Every athlete exercises self-control in all things. They do it to receive a perishable wreath, but we an imperishable" (1 Corinthians 9:24–25). We're running an imperfect race right now, but Jesus—the perfecter of our faith—will bring us across the finish line to receive an imperishable prize.

*Lord, please help me run this race to win. Amen.*

# "I Don't Understand!"

*As you do not know the way the spirit comes to the bones in the womb of a woman with child, so you do not know the work of God who makes everything.*

ECCLESIASTES 11:5

~

Some things we humans just can't explain. As much as science has advanced, God's creation is greater still. Even things we can explain are amazingly intricate. Think about all that has to happen for you to read these words—how the eyes work with the brain to make sense of marks on a page. Wise King Solomon—whom God gifted with "wisdom and understanding beyond measure, and breadth of mind like the sand on the seashore" (1 Kings 4:29)—recognized that there is a limit to what God's children are able to understand about His creation and, by extension, how He works, and Solomon shared his insight with us in Ecclesiastes 11:5. Just as we don't fully comprehend how a baby grows in the womb, we don't comprehend how God works. Or, using the footnoted wording of the verse, just as we "do not know the way of the wind," we do not know God's ways.

Is God working in your life in a way that you don't understand? Maybe you've been running in circles and wish things would straighten out. Maybe you've lost a loved one. Maybe you've received an unwanted medical diagnosis. Maybe a relationship or your job or your bank account is giving you a headache. Maybe you've stepped out on a limb for God and think you hear a crack.

Your heart cries out, *What's going on here, Lord?* Things aren't always so clear on the front line of life. We can't always make sense of what seems senseless. In the moments when we lack clarity, though, we can rest in God's omniscience. He declares, "For as the heavens are higher than the earth, so are my ways higher than your ways and my thoughts than your thoughts" (Isaiah 55:9). We may not be able to understand the how and why of what's happening, but God is able. What's more, He is in control and working for our good (Romans 8:28).

There's something else we can rest in, something else that's beyond human understanding: God's love. Paul prayed that believers would begin to understand through the Spirit "what is the width and length and depth and height—to know the love of Christ which passes knowledge" (Ephesians 3:18–19 NKJV). Yes, God works in ways we humans just can't explain, but He also loves us more than we'll ever know.

*God, I don't understand all that's happening
in my life, but I'll rest in You. Amen.*

# Cause for Boasting

*But he said to me, "My grace is sufficient for you, for my power is made perfect in weakness." Therefore I will boast all the more gladly of my weaknesses, so that the power of Christ may rest upon me.*

2 CORINTHIANS 12:9

~

Why would anyone boast in weakness? To boast is "to puff oneself up,"* after all. Our boasting goes hand in hand with our pride. We use it to show off our strengths. We don't generally drag our weaknesses into the spotlight and gush over them. They don't puff us up. So why is Paul, in his letter to the Corinthians, so glad when he's weak? Perspective is the key.

At the time Paul was writing, he was concerned about the church at Corinth. False apostles were discrediting him and undermining the Corinthians' faith by preaching a false gospel. Hoping to put an end to the threat, Paul first defended his ministry (2 Corinthians 10), and then he used the false apostles' boasting against them. What, he sarcastically questioned, could any of them boast about that he could not outdo? He was a Hebrew, a descendant of Abraham, a servant of Christ, and a better one at that, because his track record far surpassed their own (2 Corinthians 11:16–29). Yet Paul knew that such boasting was foolishness. The root of the false apostles' boasting was self; they wanted to show off what made them look good. Paul flipped this reason for boasting on its head and instead boasted in what made him look weak—like the time he made a grand escape. . .in a basket lowered through a window (2 Corinthians 11:32–33). Why the switch? The false apostles' boasting said "Look at me!" Paul's boasting said "Look at Him!" The times he was weakest pointed directly to the One who gave strength. "For the sake of Christ, then, I am content with weaknesses, insults, hardships, persecutions, and calamities," Paul wrote. "For when I am weak, then I am strong" (2 Corinthians 12:10).

Paul's view of weakness wasn't limited to its downside. The weakness itself wasn't enjoyable, but Paul saw the potential for God's power to work through him in his weakness. God told Paul, and He tells us today, that His power "is made perfect in weakness." The weaker we are, the more plainly we see how powerful God is to use even our weaknesses to His glory. Our God is mighty, and that's a reason to boast.

*God, I hate being weak. But when I feel little, I'm reminded of just how big You are. Use my weaknesses to show off Your strength. Amen.*

---

*Merriam-Webster's Collegiate Dictionary*, 11th ed. (2014), s.v. "boast."

# The Long Way Around

*When Pharaoh let the people go, God did not lead them*
*by way of the land of the Philistines, although that was near.*
*For God said, "Lest the people change their minds when*
*they see war and return to Egypt." But God led the people*
*around by the way of the wilderness toward the Red Sea.*
EXODUS 13:17–18

He called it "taking the scenic route." Wherever they were headed, the quickest way from point A to point B was not the way they went. Instead, they took back roads and made frequent stops. When the girl was young, she didn't understand what went through her father's head as he mapped out their course. Why not arrive at their destination faster? Why the delay? But as the years passed, she grew to treasure the trip. Every byway. Each roadside stand. Flat tires and all. She learned from her father as she traveled by his side. She formed memories that accompanied her no matter where life led next.

The Israelites probably didn't consider their forty-year journey through the wilderness "the scenic route." It was long, monotonous, difficult. Why not arrive at the Promised Land faster? Why the delay? While we'll never understand all that goes through God's mind (1 Corinthians 2:11), He reveals glimpses into the wisdom of His ways through the Bible. The seemingly roundabout journey to Canaan had purpose. One purpose was to ready God's people for their new lives in the land He had promised;

the wilderness was a training ground in obedience and trust, among other things. Another purpose was to ensure that Israel reached their destination. The shorter route was shorter, yes; but it was also riskier. One encounter with the Philistines, and the people would have been tempted to turn back. God was preparing a place for His people, and He would make sure they got there (Exodus 23:20).

The line between where we start and where we end up in any stage of our lives isn't always the shortest. Sometimes God takes us the roundabout way. We may wish we'd reach wherever we're headed faster. We may not even know where we're going. But once the journey is over, what a joy to look back and see God's mastery and care in action. Every road traveled, each experience, trials and all, has purpose. Even on the most winding path, we can have faith that God has a destination in mind, and He will make sure we get there.

*God, just thinking about the past few years, I'm amazed by how You got me from where I was to where I am. Thank You for the masterful way You guide me. Amen.*

# Good Question

*The angel of the Lord found her by a spring of water in
the wilderness, the spring on the way to Shur. And he said,
"Hagar, servant of Sarai, where have you come
from and where are you going?"*

GENESIS 16:7–8

∽

The child stomps to her room, propelled by huffs of displeasure and indignation. Once there, she stuffs her small suitcase with the essentials: her pajamas, her collection of seashells, her stuffed ostrich, and her stash of candy. She enters the kitchen, head held high, and declares to her mother, "I'm running away!" Maybe you starred in your own version of this scenario when you were young, or maybe you've seen it played out on TV so many times that it makes your eyes roll. Either way, most of us can identify with the child. When life chucks something at us that we're not ready—or don't want—to handle, running away seems like a pretty good option.

Hagar ran away too, but her problem was more serious than the fictitious child's. God had promised Abram and Sarai a son. Ten years later, there still was no son, so Sarai devised her own plan to fulfill God's promise. She offered her servant, Hagar, to her husband. All went according to plan; Hagar became pregnant. But what Sarai did not anticipate was Hagar's response: Hagar looked down on her. The situation continued to decline as Sarai confronted Abram, and Abram told Sarai to do as she wished with Hagar. Sarai used this freedom to mistreat Hagar so harshly that Hagar fled.

Here's where the angel of the Lord comes in. He appeared and, rather than immediately commanding Hagar to return to her mistress, asked her a question: "Where have you come from and where are you going?" In the middle of her emotions and an unbearable set of circumstances, Hagar had seen running as the best option. God asked her to pause and think it over. Of course, He already knew the answer. He knew where she had come from—and He knew where she was going. God had plans for Hagar, and He wouldn't let her stray too far from them. He saw her in the wilderness and lovingly guided her in the right direction. Hagar's response: "So she called the name of the Lord who spoke to her, 'You are a God of seeing,' for she said, 'Truly here I have seen him who looks after me' " (Genesis 16:13).

Is God asking you to pause and listen for His direction?

*Lord, lately I've been on the run, but You aren't through with Your plans for me. I'm pausing now to hear from You. . .*

# Focus!

*Set your minds on things that are above,
not on things that are on earth.*

Colossians 3:2

H er limbs trembled like wind-ruffled leaves on a tree. Her
hands were damp clamps gripping the ropes, trying both
to anchor herself and to squeeze out the fear. *Stop being so silly*,
she thought. *It's only a rope bridge.* But she couldn't get over
how far apart the boards were, and how old the ropes looked,
and how the bridge swayed with each gust of wind. Then she
looked down. *Yeah, right.* The river seemed miles below. Just
as she was about to turn on her heels and retreat, she heard her
friend's voice: "Don't look down. Keep your eyes focused on the
end of the bridge and take it one step at a time."

Having a focal point is helpful, if not crucial. Peter, for one,
could attest to that. When he saw Jesus walking on the water,
he asked to join Him, and with his eyes locked on Jesus, Peter
did the impossible. Once he looked away, however, he saw the
wind, his faith faltered, and he began to sink (Matthew 14:28–30).
While we don't walk on water a whole lot, having a focal point in
our Christian lives is still essential. Paul advised believers, "Set
your minds on things that are above, not on things that are on
earth." Why? Because Paul saw firsthand the destruction that
focusing on earthy things would cause. If, instead, believers
followed the example of those who pursued Christlikeness and

focused on heaven, they could anticipate glorious results: "Join in imitating me, and keep your eyes on those who walk according to the example you have in us. For many, of whom I have often told you and now tell you even with tears, walk as enemies of the cross of Christ. Their end is destruction, their god is their belly, and they glory in their shame, with minds set on earthly things. But our citizenship is in heaven, and from it we await a Savior, the Lord Jesus Christ, who will transform our lowly body to be like his glorious body" (Philippians 3:17–21).

In heaven, we'll be transformed, perfected. Until then, we strive to model our Savior as best we can. The earth will always be full of distractions and pitfalls, but with minds focused on "things that are above," we are filled with God's power that shapes us as His daughters day by day. Don't look down. Keep your eyes focused on heaven.

*Lord, when I take my eyes off You, I falter. So why do I let myself lose focus so easily? Please help me set my mind on things above. Amen.*

# Our Defense

*Submit yourselves therefore to God. Resist the devil,*
*and he will flee from you. Draw near to God,*
*and he will draw near to you.*
JAMES 4:7–8

eter did not mince words when he warned believers about a danger of the Christian life: "Be sober-minded; be watchful. Your adversary the devil prowls around like a roaring lion, seeking someone to devour" (1 Peter 5:8). Paul also wrote in strong terms of the opposition confronting believers: "For we do not wrestle against flesh and blood, but against the rulers, against the authorities, against the cosmic powers over this present darkness, against the spiritual forces of evil in the heavenly places" (Ephesians 6:12). *Okay then.* Like it or not, we're at war—in a spiritual battle. There's a reason Satan and his forces are called the enemy. His goal is to see us defeated.

Not coincidentally, we often feel the devil strike the hardest when we are doing our best to live a godly life. If a person is already straying from God, she's right where the devil wants her. But when she's walking God's way? The devil aims to slow her down, detour her, or stop her in her tracks. Sometimes it seems as if making a decision to follow God more closely opens the door for an all-out assault as the devil tries to undermine our efforts.

One of his tactics is to convince us through lies that God is not present. Maybe you've heard some of them: "Still waiting on an answer to that prayer? That's because God isn't listening"; "All the 'bad' in your life right now just proves that God doesn't care"; "Why would God bother to do anything for *you*?" Lies, every last one. So how do we fight them?

Our defense against any and all of Satan's tactics comes from almighty God: "Be strong in the Lord and in the strength of his might. Put on the whole armor of God, that you may be able to stand against the schemes of the devil" (Ephesians 6:10–11). Daily we put on God's armor. Daily we resist the devil. Daily, even hourly, we choose to say, "I trust in God." If you think you're not up to the fight, remember, the One who is in us is far greater than the devil (1 John 4:4). God is with us each time we face the enemy, each time we say, "I trust in You." When we place ourselves in God's hands, taking a stand against the devil, the devil has no choice but to run.

*Father, I'm afraid of the battle, but Your Word encourages me. With You as my defense, I don't have to fight the devil alone. Amen.*

# Even That One

*He is the propitiation for our sins, and not for ours*
*only but also for the sins of the whole world.*
1 JOHN 2:2

❧

The dishcloth had been in commission for years. After rinsing the last of a sinkful of pots and pans, the woman looked down at the grimy, soppy, ratty piece of cloth. To wash or to toss? Into the trash can it went; it was beyond redemption. Sin can make us feel like that dishrag at times. Whether because of sin that caught us unawares or a temptation we've struggled with over and over, we may wonder if we're beyond redemption. Surely God won't forgive *this one*.

Where does this type of thinking come from? It begins with an inflated view of ourselves and a deficient view of Christ's sacrifice. To think that we were slightly more redeemable before one sin or another is to give ourselves credit we don't deserve. To think that Christ's death covers some sin but not all is to limit His righteousness. In reality, we all fall short of God's holy standard (Romans 3:23), and to fall short by even the slightest margin makes us unworthy of heaven. But Jesus' death is sufficient to save everyone, completely: "For Christ also died for sins once for all, the just for the unjust, so that He might bring us to God" (1 Peter 3:18 NASB).

Still not convinced? Consider these words from Paul: "We ourselves were once foolish, disobedient, led astray, slaves to various passions and pleasures. . . . But when the goodness and loving kindness of God our Savior appeared, he saved us, not because of works done by us in righteousness, but according to his own mercy, by the washing of regeneration and renewal of the Holy Spirit, whom he poured out on us richly through Jesus Christ our Savior" (Titus 3:3–6). God, in a gesture that displayed His vast love for us when we were far from worthy, reached down and offered salvation. He offered to remove our sin—to wash us, renew us—through the righteousness of His Son. We were never too grimy, soppy, or ratty for God to make us clean and whole.

We're still not. God's forgiveness is always available. "If we confess our sins," says 1 John, "he is faithful and just to forgive us our sins, and to cleanse us from *all* unrighteousness" (1:9 KJV, emphasis added). God is faithful to forgive. . .even that one.

*God, I've sinned. Right now I feel so undeserving of Your forgiveness. But I know I am Your child; Christ's righteousness is my own. Forgive this sin. Please wash me clean again. Amen.*

# You 2.0

*Therefore we do not lose heart. Though outwardly we are wasting away, yet inwardly we are being renewed day by day. For our light and momentary troubles are achieving for us an eternal glory that far outweighs them all.*

2 CORINTHIANS 4:16–17 NIV

~

nothing lasts forever; it's true, and our earthly bodies are no exception. They are prone to illness and injury. Joints stiffen, skin wrinkles, hair grays, muscles weaken with age. The troubles that go along with living bruise us time and again. But as Paul told the Corinthians, don't lose heart. As Christians, we know this body—this life—is not the end. We don't have a handful of years on earth and then nothing. We look forward to an eternity of years in heaven.

Although these physical bodies—the flesh and blood and bones that make us human—are only temporary, God still cares about them. Jesus, who experienced all the frailties of a human body, has compassion for us, and He often healed physical ailments as part of His earthly ministry. Yet the physical healing was just the beginning and a symbol of something greater. Matthew wrote of Jesus' healing, "This was to fulfill what was spoken by the prophet Isaiah: 'He took our illnesses and bore our diseases' " (Matthew 8:17). Jesus' death allowed us to be healed body *and* soul. "He was pierced for our transgressions; he was crushed for our iniquities; upon him was the chastisement that brought us peace, and with his wounds we are healed" (Isaiah 53:5). Because of Jesus, we have a cure for the sickness inside—the invisible disease called sin that leads to death—and the promise of perfected bodies in heaven, where both sin and sickness will be eradicated.

Paul had more to tell the Corinthians: "In this [tent, our physical body] we groan, earnestly desiring to be clothed with our habitation which is from heaven. . . . For we who are in this tent groan, being burdened, not because we want to be unclothed, but further clothed, that mortality may be swallowed up by life. Now He who has prepared us for this very thing is God, who also has given us the Spirit as a guarantee. So we are always confident" (2 Corinthians 5:2, 4–6 NKJV).

For now we have these bodies to deal with—the outer self and its wasting away. But we don't lose heart. God is renewing our inner self. Through this life He is preparing us for something greater.

*Lord, thank You for caring about the whole me.*
*When I'm hurting physically, You hear my prayers to*
*heal this body of mine. But far better than that—*
*You have already healed my soul. Amen.*

# "Tell Me What to Say"

*"Do not be anxious beforehand what you are
to say, but say whatever is given you in that hour,
for it is not you who speak, but the Holy Spirit."*
MARK 13:11

At a loss for words. Have you ever been there? A situation is so surprising, overwhelming, or intimidating that when you open your mouth, all you can manage is silence?

The disciples likely could imagine a time when they wouldn't know what to say. Peter, James, John, and Andrew were on the Mount of Olives with Jesus, and Jesus had just foretold the destruction of the temple. In response, the disciples asked about the end times. What Jesus divulged would make even the bravest believer tremble in his sandals. Jesus spoke of false prophets, wars, earthquakes, famines, pestilences, and terrors (Matthew 24:4–8; Mark 13:5–8; Luke 21:8–11). On top of all that, there would be persecution. Believers would be abused and brought before religious and government leaders to bear witness (Mark 13:9; Luke 21:12–13). A blank mind—or, at the very least, doubt about the adequacy of their response—would be natural under the circumstances. Knowing that His words would cause concern, Jesus paired them with some instructions and a promise. Jesus told believers not to be anxious about what to say. Why? Because the Holy Spirt would speak through them. Again in Luke, Jesus said, "Settle it therefore in your minds not to meditate beforehand how to answer, for I will give you a mouth and wisdom, which none of your adversaries will be able to withstand or contradict" (Luke 21:14–15).

Jesus' assurance of divine assistance might have reminded the disciples of another incident from generations past. When God commissioned Moses to lead Israel out of Egypt, Moses had a number of excuses why he wasn't fit for the job, the fourth being that his lack of eloquence would fail to convince Pharaoh of anything. God's response nixed that argument: "Who has made man's mouth? . . . Is it not I, the LORD? Now therefore go, and I will be with your mouth and teach you what you shall speak" (Exodus 4:11–12).

Even if we don't face a pharaoh or the persecution Jesus spoke about, we still may worry that we'll be at a loss for words when it matters. What about defending our faith when others mock us? What about sharing the Gospel with a dear friend? In those times, we have the Holy Spirit to help us find just the right words.

*God, I worry that I won't know what to say about my faith if I'm put on the spot. Please reassure me of Your presence and power. Amen.*

# Choose Your God

*And Elijah came near to all the people and said,
"How long will you go limping between two different
opinions? If the LORD is God, follow him;
but if Baal, then follow him."*
1 KINGS 18:21

⁓

A carved wooden figure. An altar dedicated to a god of harvest, or fertility, or rain. . . That's what we think of as idols, right? We might even skim over the Bible's passages on idolatry and say, "Not for me!" Those passages were full of truth and relevance in Old Testament times, we don't doubt, but today? Not so much. Yet Israel's struggle isn't so far removed from our own.

Israel was on dangerous ground. Although they had not rejected God completely, as Baalism spread, God's people began combining worship of the Lord with worship of Baal. Enter Elijah. God sent the prophet to challenge Baalism, to warn Israel that they could not continue "limping between" two choices. Almighty God would not accept a part-time place on the throne of their hearts. If God was their God, they needed to follow Him alone.

God's warnings against idolatry are not reserved for the false gods of the Old Testament. It's just as vital for us today that God takes His rightful place in our lives. In the Sermon on the Mount, Jesus told the crowd, "No one can serve two masters, for either he will hate the one and love the other, or he will be devoted to the one and despise the other" (Matthew 6:24). As believers, we cannot hop between devotion to God and devotion to earthly things. We cannot split the role of "God" between God and our bank account—or our possessions, our romantic life, our family, our beauty, our career goals—and expect to get anywhere. If God is our God, we must follow Him alone, serving and worshipping Him exclusively.

"There are many 'gods' and many 'lords,' " Paul wrote the Corinthians, "yet for us there is one God, the Father, from whom are all things and for whom we exist, and one Lord, Jesus Christ" (1 Corinthians 8:5–6). He then issued a warning: "Let anyone who thinks that he stands take heed lest he fall. . . . Therefore, my beloved, flee from idolatry" (1 Corinthians 10:12, 14). Christians today are not immune to idols. If anything, they might be harder to spot since we don't often physically bow down to them. Before we dismiss the warnings as "Not for me," let's look closely at our lives. What is taking God's rightful place?

*God, I'm so ashamed. Lately I've been living as if You aren't God in my life. Forgive me, please. Dethrone my idols and reign fully in me. Amen.*

# Back to Him

*[Hannah] was deeply distressed and prayed to the LORD and wept bitterly. And she vowed a vow and said, "O LORD of hosts, if you will indeed look on the affliction of your servant and remember me and not forget your servant, but will give to your servant a son, then I will give him to the LORD all the days of his life."*
1 SAMUEL 1:10–11

Think about a time when you desperately asked for God to fulfill a deep need in your life. Not just a run-of-the-mill "It would be nice if God grants my request," but an honest-to-goodness "I'd give an arm and a leg for God to grant my request." In all your praying, did it cross your mind to offer back to God the thing you prayed for? If it didn't, you're not alone. We might think to offer something else. We might promise to do something in return. But release what we've prayed for? That says a great deal, and that's exactly what Hannah did.

Hannah desperately wanted a son. Although she had the love of her husband, Elkanah, her status as a woman in her culture hinged on the children she bore. Add to that the fact that her husband's second wife, Peninnah, regularly tormented Hannah because of her barrenness, and you begin to see what a son meant to Hannah. So on one of their yearly trips to Shiloh to worship and sacrifice, Hannah went to the temple to pray. There Hannah poured out her soul (1 Samuel 1:15). So intense was her plea that Eli, the priest at the temple, thought she was drunk. But she was only approaching her heavenly Father in raw humility and with deep faith.

Hannah's prayer was for a son, as one would expect, but her prayer was also a promise to take what God gave and give it right back to Him. Her blessings came from God, and back to God they would go. In all aspects of her life, it seems, Hannah recognized the Source. Hannah left the temple that day heartened. The Bible says "her face was no longer sad" (1 Samuel 1:18). How could that be? On the surface, nothing had changed; she still did not have a son. But she had placed her need in the hands of her God, and Hannah trusted in His providence. The One who had closed her womb (verse 5) was in control and was completely capable of answering her prayer favorably with the birth of a son. And so He would.

*Lord, sometimes I lose You in my prayers. I hyperfocus on me and forget to look beyond to You. How can I give back from all You've given me? Please show me. Amen.*

# Fruitful

*But the fruit of the Spirit is love, joy, peace,*
*patience, kindness, goodness, faithfulness, gentleness,*
*self-control; against such things there is no law.*
GALATIANS 5:22–23

❧

If it looks like a duck, swims like a duck, and quacks like a duck, then it's probably. . .a duck!" Whether you've heard some version of this expression or not, the conclusion is obvious. If something is that something, it generally exhibits certain characteristics. That goes for people as well as ducks. Take, for instance, believers. If a Christian is a Christian, she will exhibit certain characteristics—what Paul called "the fruit of the Spirit."

When we become believers, God gifts us with the Holy Spirit (Acts 2:38), and the Spirit's presence is one way we can reassure ourselves of our salvation (1 John 4:13). He is much more than a token proof, though. The Holy Spirit becomes our power source to resist the flesh and live a godly life. The fruit—the love, joy, peace, patience, kindness, goodness, faithfulness, gentleness, and self-control listed in Galatians—is evidence of His working. Jesus, in His Sermon on the Mount, described the opposite when He warned the crowd to be on guard against those who claimed to know the way to salvation but did not. "Beware of false prophets, who come to you in sheep's clothing but inwardly are ravenous wolves," He said. How could they tell a true shepherd from a wolf? "You will recognize them by their fruits. Are grapes gathered from thornbushes, or figs from thistles? So, every healthy tree bears good fruit, but the diseased tree bears bad fruit. A healthy tree cannot bear bad fruit, nor can a diseased tree bear good fruit. . . . Thus you will recognize them by their fruits" (Matthew 7:15–18, 20). True believers, because of the Holy Spirit, will bear good fruit.

So what is a Christian like? She's loving—showing the kind of love Christ showed. She's joyful—possessing a sense of well-being from God no matter the circumstance. She's peaceful—resting in the calm of knowing God. She's patient—long-suffering through hardships. She's kind—treating others with care and concern. She's good—displaying the holiness fitting for one of God's children. She's faithful—proving herself trustworthy, devoted. She's gentle—having a spirit of meekness. She's self-controlled—taming the flesh while pursuing godliness.

However small the harvest, the Holy Spirit is producing what we could not produce alone. May it be our prayer that we bear more and more of that good fruit.

*Holy Spirit, I see the fruit You yield in my life. It's my desire to bear a bounty of good fruit—so much that others see me and say, "That's a Christian!" Amen.*

# Share the Comfort

*Blessed be the God and Father of our Lord Jesus Christ,
the Father of mercies and God of all comfort, who comforts
us in all our affliction, so that we may be able to comfort
those who are in any affliction, with the comfort with
which we ourselves are comforted by God.*

2 Corinthians 1:3–4

It's a friend who sits beside us for hours on the hard waiting-room chairs. It's the gentle embrace of Mom or Dad rocking us back to sleep when we were young. It's heads huddled together while we talk over our troubles. It's the outstretched hand that lets us know we don't have to walk alone. Comfort takes many forms, but it often involves the support of someone else.

In the Bible, another name for the Holy Spirit, our Comforter, is Paraclete. The name derives from the Greek word *Paraklētos*, which can be translated "advocate" or "intercessor." Like a lawyer who stands beside a defendant in a court case, the Holy Spirit comes alongside believers in life—counseling them, helping them. No wonder the word for "comfort" that Paul used in 2 Corinthians is related to the Greek *paraclete*. Paul had experienced intense struggle in Asia—to such a degree that he felt he had "received the sentence of death" (2 Corinthians 1:9). Yet through it all, Paul was convinced of God's presence—upholding him, encouraging him, and, ultimately, delivering him. He was convinced too of the surety of God's comfort, that even in the most intense situation, God's comfort abounded, both for himself and for fellow believers: "For just as the sufferings of Christ are ours in abundance, so also our comfort is abundant through Christ. But if we are afflicted, it is for your comfort and salvation; or if we are comforted, it is for your comfort. . .and our hope for you is firmly grounded, knowing that as you are sharers of our sufferings, so also you are sharers of our comfort" (2 Corinthians 1:5–7 NASB).

Paul knew one other truth about God's comfort. The benefits went beyond the immediate comfort itself. Each instance of God's comfort in the midst of suffering bolstered faith and united believers. And once comforted by God themselves, believers in turn could comfort others. The same rich layering of comfort continues to this day. In the midst of our sufferings, God comes alongside us—upholding us, encouraging us, and delivering us. We in turn have the joy of sharing the blessing of His comfort.

*God, You never stop comforting me. You are always with me to help me through my struggles. Remind me to share with others the endless ways You work in my life. Amen.*

# Cast Those Cares!

*Casting all your anxieties on him,*
*because he cares for you.*
1 PETER 5:7

A belly of nerves has to be one of the most uncomfortable feelings there is. You're on edge. Your mind won't settle except on what you're uneasy about, which it cycles over and over. And the more you feed anxiety, the quicker you are to become anxious. When we're feeling anxious, we easily forget that anxiety itself isn't always bad. The sudden unease caused by a cracking twig when we're walking alone or an unfamiliar creak of the floorboards at night alerts us to potential danger. We're revved up for a reason. . .until the danger passes. But we simply aren't meant to be anxious about every little thing, every waking moment.

Yet we often are, and we're not the first generation to need an anxiety cure. Our propensity for anxiety is age-old. Back in Bible times, Jesus had a few words to say on the subject, and He also nudged us toward the solution: "Consider the lilies of the field, how they grow: they neither toil nor spin, yet I tell you, even Solomon in all his glory was not arrayed like one of these. But if God so clothes the grass of the field, which today is alive and tomorrow is thrown into the oven, will he not much more clothe you, O you of little faith? Therefore do not be anxious, saying, 'What shall we eat?' or 'What shall we drink?' or 'What shall we wear?' . . . Your heavenly Father knows that you need them all" (Matthew 6:28–32). What's the antidote to anxiety? Reminding ourselves of God's presence in our lives and trusting Him to take care of us.

"Blessed is the man who trusts in the LORD," God said. "He is like a tree planted by water, that. . .is not anxious in the year of drought, for it does not cease to bear fruit" (Jeremiah 17:7–8). No matter what our circumstances, we can trade the unsettledness of anxiety for the assurance of God's care. We can surrender our worries to the One who gives life. "Cast your burden on the LORD, and He shall sustain you" (Psalm 55:22 NKJV). Peter echoes the psalmist's words, telling believers to cast their anxieties on God. Don't miss the vivid language in these verses. *Cast* your burden, your anxieties. With each anxious thought, picture your heavenly Father and cast those cares over His shoulders. Because He knows what to do with them. Because He cares for you.

*Lord, I cast all that's twisting me up inside on You. You'll take care of me. Amen.*

# Drastic Measures

*"And if your hand or your foot causes you to sin, cut it off and throw it away. It is better for you to enter life crippled or lame than with two hands or two feet to be thrown into the eternal fire. And if your eye causes you to sin, tear it out and throw it away. It is better for you to enter life with one eye than with two eyes to be thrown into the hell of fire."*

MATTHEW 18:8–9

What's the best policy when it comes to dealing with sin? Nip it in the bud. You've likely heard that expression before. It means to halt something early on and refers to new flower buds that a spring frost kills before they have a chance to grow.

Jesus used a more arresting depiction of how to deal with sin. And He used it more than once (Matthew 5:29–30; 18:8–9). If a person's hand, foot, or eye causes her to sin, it is better to lose that hand, foot, or eye than suffer the consequences of sin. Of course, He was exaggerating to make a point. He wasn't advocating that we harm our bodies to manage sin in our lives. Punishing the outside won't begin to touch the source of sin in our hearts. But when dealing with a temptation to sin, it is best to get rid of it completely, rather than flirt with the temptation and risk sinning.

Whether we realize it or not, we Christians are at risk of adopting a destructive mind-set. With Christ's death on the cross, He paid the penalty for our sins, every last one. If we sin and repent, God will forgive, every single time. So is sin still a big deal? Yes! Here's what Paul wrote on the issue: "What shall we say then? Shall we continue in sin that grace may abound? Certainly not! . . . Therefore do not let sin reign in your mortal body, that you should obey it in its lusts. And do not present your members as instruments of unrighteousness to sin, but present yourselves to God as being alive from the dead, and your members as instruments of righteousness to God" (Romans 6:1–2, 12–13 NKJV). Forgiveness is not a license to sin; neither is sin beneficial to a believer. If we want to be used by God to the fullest and grow in Him, we must deal with sin. Christ took drastic measures to free us. At the first sign of temptation, let's do the same and nip sin in the bud.

*Lord, the next time I face temptation, remind me of Your sacrifice. Help me rid my life of anything that causes me to sin. Amen.*

*At that time the disciples came to Jesus, saying, "Who is the greatest in the kingdom of heaven?" And calling to him a child, he put him in the midst of them and said, "Truly, I say to you, unless you turn and become like children, you will never enter the kingdom of heaven. Whoever humbles himself like this child is the greatest in the kingdom of heaven."*

Matthew 18:1–4

That was just too easy! What am I missing?" she said.

What is it about simple things that makes us question them? Sometimes complexity only adds complexity. Just look at the reams of paper that are the US tax code. It's true for religion too. The Pharisees were famous for complicating God's law with added regulations. But when Jesus arrived on the scene, He preached a way to righteousness through faith that defied complexity.

It wasn't the outwardly religious but inwardly unchanged Pharisees, or even one of His devoted followers, to whom Jesus pointed in answer to the disciples' question of who was "greatest in the kingdom." It was a child. At another time, parents brought their children to Jesus so He could bless them. Although the disciples tried to turn them away, Jesus welcomed the children. "Let the children come to me," He said. "Do not hinder them, for to such belongs the kingdom of God. Truly, I say to you, whoever does not receive the kingdom of God like a child shall not enter it" (Mark 10:14–15). To Jesus, the child embodied what all the "stuff" of religion could never produce: the pure heart and faith of a child in relationship with the Father. A child with nothing to offer but everything to gain. A child full of trust in her Father for every need. A child content to rest at her Father's knee.

We, as God's children, should come to the Father in the same way. To deepen our faith, we must simplify our faith. As A. W. Tozer wrote, "Now, as always, God discovers Himself to 'babes' and hides Himself in thick darkness from the wise and the prudent. We must simplify our approach to Him. We must strip down to essentials (and they will be found to be blessedly few). We must put away all effort to impress and come with the guileless candor of childhood. If we do this, without doubt God will quickly respond."*

*God, I'm tired of running in circles, of complicating faith and feeling no closer to You. Today I call to You— daughter to heavenly Father. Amen.*

---

*A. W. Tozer, *The Pursuit of God* (Chicago: Moody Publishers, 2015), 24.

# Times Infinity

*"Judge not, and you will not be judged; condemn not, and you will not be condemned; forgive, and you will be forgiven; give, and it will be given to you. Good measure, pressed down, shaken together, running over, will be put into your lap. For with the measure you use it will be measured back to you."*

LUKE 6:37–38

This had happened before. Like a bad dream on rerun, once more her friend had wronged her. She knew what to do—forgive. But she knew the feeling seeping into her heart too—hardness. She'd forgiven time and again; had she finally reached her limit?

Questions about forgiveness are nothing new. Even the disciples questioned just how far to extend forgiveness. When Peter asked Jesus to clarify, he also threw out a number that he must have thought generous: "Lord, how often shall my brother sin against me, and I forgive him? Up to seven times?" But Jesus' reply declared that seven times was just the beginning: "I do not say to you, up to seven times, but up to seventy times seven" (Matthew 18:21–22 NKJV). In other words, innumerable times. A limitless number.

Our model for limitless forgiveness is God's forgiveness. The debt we owed because of sin was unpayable, and we didn't deserve a pardon. But on the cross, Christ paid our debt in full.

He called out for our forgiveness before we knew our need, just as He did for His tormentors at His crucifixion. Even in His agony, His hope for condemned sinners was forgiveness: "Father, forgive them, for they know not what they do" (Luke 23:34). By believing in Jesus, complete forgiveness from the final penalty for sin—eternity separated from God—is ours. Righteousness is ours. "We have been sanctified through the offering of the body of Jesus Christ once for all" (Hebrews 10:10).

Such total, blessed forgiveness is not the extent of God's forgiving nature, either. The One who has pardoned an unpayable debt continues to forgive us when we disobey. Even with the best intentions, we will still fail time and again, and time and again we can ask our Father's forgiveness without crossing our fingers that He'll forgive. He will. Hardening our hearts and refusing to offer forgiveness does not honor God's grace, and He won't overlook our stinginess, a scenario that Jesus illustrated in His parable of the unforgiving servant (Matthew 18:23–35). But when we forgive generously, limitlessly, as God does, we will get back an equal measure.

*Father, You have forgiven me too many times to count. When I struggle to forgive just one more time, help me forgive again, and again. May my forgiveness point the way to Yours. Amen.*

# Take a Look Around

*The heavens declare the glory of God,*
*and the sky above proclaims his handiwork.*
PSALM 19:1

❧

**W**ant to hear about God? Step outside. The heavens are declaring, the sky is proclaiming the truth about the Creator. Nature shouts how awesome God is—from the tip-top of the sky to the deepest depths of the ocean.

What God reveals about Himself through His creation is called general revelation (as opposed to special revelation—what God reveals to individual people directly), and it is available to everyone, at every moment. David continued in his psalm, "Day to day pours out speech, and night to night reveals knowledge. There is no speech, nor are there words, whose voice is not heard. Their voice goes out through all the earth, and their words to the end of the world" (Psalm 19:2–4). Paul, when explaining why those who tried to suppress the truth about God and dwell in their sinfulness were without excuse, used nature's testimony. God's witness was all around people: "What can be known about God is plain to them, because God has shown it to them. For his invisible attributes, namely, his eternal power and divine nature, have been clearly perceived, ever since the creation of the world, in the things that have been made" (Romans 1:19–20).

If we take the time to listen and observe, we can't miss God speaking through nature. Jonathan Edwards, the theologian at the root of the Great Awakening, could attest to that. After his spiritual transformation, he saw ever more of his Creator in the world around him: "My sense of divine things gradually increased, and became more and more lively, and had more of that inward sweetness. . . . God's excellency, his wisdom, his purity and love, seemed to appear in everything; in the sun, moon and stars; in the clouds, and blue sky; in the grass, flowers, trees; in the water, and all nature."*

There's no better place to look for reassurance of God's presence and power than nature. Can we see the intricacy of a snowflake, the hues of a sunset, or the lush growth of plants without imagining a Creator? Can we hear the boom of thunder, the rush of waves, or the silence of a vast night sky without thinking of Someone higher than ourselves? God's creation is shouting. The same almighty God at work in nature is at work in us.

*God, in my modern life, I've lost something of You. Even if it's only a few minutes, I want to set aside time every day to hear what Your creation has to say. Amen.*

*Quoted in George M. Marsden, *Jonathan Edwards: A Life* (New Haven, CT: Yale University Press, 2003), chap. 3.

# Anywhere at All

*If I take the wings of the morning and dwell in the uttermost parts of the sea, even there your hand shall lead me, and your right hand shall hold me.*
PSALM 139:9–10

～

She sat on a park bench watching the pedestrians and drivers on the busy sidewalks and streets around her. Her brain began to churn: What were their names? What were their stories? Where were they headed? And this cityscape was only one small patch of the planet! In that moment, thinking of all the billions of other lives spread across the globe, she could have felt tiny, like just another face in humanity's crowd. But instead she felt a rush of wonder—because in that moment, she also thought of God watching over her.

Now and then, we can lose sight of God in our lives or even question whether He's there. When we fade into daily routine or face difficult times, we may think, *Does God see me?* Yet no matter what our heads say, we can reassure our hearts with the truth from God's Word:

*Wherever we find ourselves, God hasn't lost track of us.* Quicker than a breath, God can pinpoint His own—zooming in from heaven to our world to our country to our city to our street to a park bench—and He is intimately aware of everything in our lives. In Psalm 139—a testament to God's "omni-" attributes, His omniscience, omnipresence, and omnipotence—David wrote,

"O Lord, you have searched me and known me! You know when I sit down and when I rise up; you discern my thoughts from afar. You search out my path and my lying down and are acquainted with all my ways" (verses 1–3).

*Wherever we go, God is there.* Nothing we do is out of God's sight because He is present everywhere. "Where shall I go from your Spirit? Or where shall I flee from your presence?" David asked. "If I ascend to heaven, you are there! If I make my bed in Sheol, you are there!" (verses 7–8).

*And wherever God is, He is at work.* David had sensed God forming his path throughout his life—"You hem me in, behind and before, and lay your hand upon me" (verse 5)—so he had confidence that even "in the uttermost parts of the sea," God's hand would guide and keep him (verses 9–10). That confidence is ours too. God's mighty hand is guiding us and will never let go.

*God, I'm awestruck by You! I'm only one in many billions, but You know me so well. Thank You for watching over my life—where I am today and wherever I'll be tomorrow. Amen.*

# Still with Us

*All this took place to fulfill what the Lord had spoken by the prophet: "Behold, the virgin shall conceive and bear a son, and they shall call his name Immanuel"*
*(which means, God with us).*
MATTHEW 1:22–23

⁓

Picture God. What image do you have in your mind's eye? Is He a white-haired, bearded man like the one in Michelangelo's fresco at the Sistine Chapel? Is He a nebulous form? Is He a blank? Your first thought might not have been a baby in a manger, a boy on the streets of Nazareth, a man on the way to the cross.

No one has seen God (John 1:18; 1 John 4:12), but in a miracle that humans could never dream up and only God could bring about, God made Himself known through Jesus—deity in a mortal body. Immanuel—God with us. John wrote in his Gospel, "And the Word became flesh and dwelt among us, and we have seen his glory, glory as of the only Son from the Father" (John 1:14). With the birth of Jesus, humanity had access to God like never before as the One who created everything spent time among His creation, as the embodiment of the fullness of God left heaven to walk this earth.

Jesus' earthly life was no vacation, a quick jaunt to look around. Fully God, He was also fully man, and He experienced what we experience. He felt joy and sorrow, health and sickness, comfort and pain, strength and weakness. But unlike us, He lived a perfect life from start to finish. He faced temptation and endured so that we could claim His perfection as our own. He hungered and thirsted and bled and died for our sake.

Each day, we walk this earth as imperfect beings. We're not yet who we'll be in eternity. But each day, we walk with the assurance that God, who was with us on earth, has compassion on us, and we can call on Him in our need (Hebrews 4:15–16). Even though Immanuel has returned to heaven for a time and no longer dwells among us, we are never without God. Before His final days, Jesus comforted His disciples with the promise of the Holy Spirit, and it is our promise too: "[The Father] will give you another Helper, to be with you forever, even the Spirit of truth, whom the world cannot receive, because it neither sees him nor knows him. You know him, for he dwells with you and will be in you" (John 14:16–17).

*God, thank You—for Your Son who dwelled among us until He made a way to You, and for Your Spirit who dwells in us until we're forever with You. Amen.*

# Get Ready

*Now there was one, Anna, a prophetess, the daughter of*
*Phanuel, of the tribe of Asher. She was of a great age,*
*and had lived with a husband seven years from her virginity;*
*and this woman was a widow of about eighty-four years,*
*who did not depart from the temple, but served God with*
*fastings and prayers night and day. And coming in that*
*instant she gave thanks to the Lord, and spoke of Him*
*to all those who looked for redemption in Jerusalem.*

LUKE 2:36–38 NKJV

❧

Jesus was only weeks old. In keeping with the law of Moses, Joseph and Mary traveled from Bethlehem to Jerusalem to present Him at the temple and offer a sacrifice. Waiting for them was Simeon, a righteous and devout man with a promise: he would not die before he had seen Christ. So on the day Joseph and Mary brought Jesus to Jerusalem, Simeon was also there. The Bible says he "came in the Spirit into the temple" (Luke 2:27). Spirit-led Simeon knew right away who the infant was. In what must have been great joy, Simeon "took him up in his arms and blessed God and said, 'Lord, now you are letting your servant depart in peace, according to your word; for my eyes have seen your salvation that you have prepared in the presence of all peoples, a light for revelation to the Gentiles, and for glory to your people Israel' " (Luke 2:28–32). While Simeon was still praising and blessing, a woman entered the scene in the perfect timing of her Lord. "Coming in that instant" was Anna.

It's just a guess, but Anna's life at eighty-four probably didn't look like what she had imagined as a young girl. Married then widowed after seven years, she now was a prophetess—"a woman who spoke God's Word"*—and lived at the temple. Evidently, Anna did not let early widowhood dampen her faith but continued to serve her Lord faithfully. Night and day she fasted and prayed, readying her heart for what God called her to. And night and day, God was present behind the scenes in Anna's life and the lives of those around her. From Jesus' birth to Joseph and Mary's trip to Simeon's words, God was laying the foundation to bless and work through Anna at exactly the right moment—the moment when Anna saw the fulfillment of her faith in person and then went on to tell others that Messiah was here.

*Lord, life isn't always what I imagined it would be. But I'll have faith that You are preparing the way for something better than I could imagine. Amen.*

---

*John MacArthur, *The MacArthur Bible Commentary* (Nashville: Thomas Nelson, 2005), 1279.

# Faithful Giving

*Whoever brings blessing will be enriched.*
PROVERBS 11:25

R eady for a tough question? When it comes to giving of yourself—whether it's your time or your resources—where are you on the giving scale? Do you grip what you have to give and only let a little trickle out through your fingers? Do you offer everything with open hands? Maybe you're somewhere in between. If the number of times the Bible speaks of generosity is any indication, we all need to work on cultivating a generous heart.

Both Mark and Luke record a memorable lesson on giving (Mark 12:41–44; Luke 21:1–4). Jesus was watching the people bring their offerings, and among the rich with their large sums of money, He saw her: a poor widow who dropped a couple of small coins into the offering box. Jesus gathered His disciples and said, "Truly, I tell you, this poor widow has put in more than all of them. For they all contributed out of their abundance, but she out of her poverty put in all she had to live on" (Luke 21:3–4). The widow's offering did not amount to a day's wage, but Jesus honored her gift because great faith underlaid her generosity. She gave her last cent, trusting God to provide her every last need.

How do we cultivate generous hearts? By growing our faith. "The point is this," Paul wrote; "whoever sows sparingly will also reap sparingly, and whoever sows bountifully will also reap bountifully. Each one must give as he has decided in his heart, not reluctantly or under compulsion, for God loves a cheerful giver. And God is able to make all grace abound to you, so that having all sufficiency in all things at all times, you may abound in every good work. . . . You will be enriched in every way to be generous in every way" (2 Corinthians 9:6–8, 11). Believers would abound in every good work and be generous in every way because God would supply and God would enrich. The kind of wholesale giving Paul wrote the Corinthians about pointed to the One the giver relied on for the seeds to sow (verse 10). "It is a proof of your faith," he told them (2 Corinthians 9:13 NCV).

Put your faith in God and give generously and He *will* be faithful. "Test Me now in this," the Lord told Israel, "if I will not open for you the windows of heaven and pour out for you a blessing until it overflows" (Malachi 3:10 NASB).

*God, forgive me for the times I've held on to blessings because I've lacked faith. You will always give more than I can give away. Amen.*

## Quenched

*And the LORD will guide you continually and satisfy your desire in scorched places. . .and you shall be like a watered garden, like a spring of water, whose waters do not fail.*

ISAIAH 58:11

⟡

The land was all dust and dryness. A sea of sand-colored earth stretched out as far as sight. But across the parched ground were dots of color, splashes of life. Tiny wildflowers were blooming.

If you've ever seen plants growing in the desert, you might marvel at their ability to thrive in an arid climate. And if you are experiencing some sort of drought in your life—whether you're sapped physically or drained emotionally or dried up spiritually—you might envy them. With cracked dirt below, the glaring sun above, and so little rain falling between, how do they still grow?

The biblical writers often used images of plant life to describe a godly person, with an emphasis on an ability to thrive—to remain green and fruitful—even in difficult times. In the book of Psalms, the godly person "is like a tree planted by streams of water that yields its fruit in its season, and its leaf does not wither" (Psalm 1:3). Jeremiah compared the godly to "a tree planted by water, that sends out its roots by the stream, and does not fear when heat comes, for its leaves remain green, and is not anxious in the year of drought, for it does not cease to bear fruit" (Jeremiah 17:8). What is this source of water that keeps the godly man (or woman) growing? "His delight is in the law of the LORD, and on his law he meditates day and night," the psalmist said (Psalm 1:2). And " 'Blessed is the man who trusts in the LORD, whose trust is the LORD,' " wrote Jeremiah (Jeremiah 17:7).

God provides a constant source of life-giving water to the believer. Jesus declared, "Whoever believes in me, as the Scripture has said, 'Out of his heart will flow rivers of living water' " (John 7:37–38). God's living water both grants eternal life in heaven and supports spiritual life on earth through the Spirit. We as believers need water to grow just as we need air to breathe. Perhaps this truth is most obvious when we're in a dry spell. It's then that we cry out like the psalmist, "As the deer pants for the water brooks, so pants my soul for You, O God. My soul thirsts for God, for the living God" (Psalm 42:1–2 NKJV).

When you're thirsty, return to the Source. Dip deeply into God's Word. Drink your fill of His presence.

*Holy Spirit, fill me to the brim with living water. Amen.*

# Persistently Persistent

*And he told them a parable to the effect that they ought always to pray and not lose heart.*

LUKE 18:1

**D**addy?"

*Here it comes*, thought the father while holding back a grin. "What is it, honey?"

"Can I have a surfboard?"

"Maybe."

"I'd take good care of it. Can't I get one, please?"

"Maybe."

"But I've asked a bazillion times. Please, please, please?"

"Ask me one more time and we'll see."

If you ever asked for something over and over as a child, you remember how difficult the waiting was, but you probably didn't hesitate to ask. Is the same true with your heavenly Father? Are you as bold to ask over and over in your prayers to Him?

Persistence in prayer isn't frowned on in the Bible. In fact, Jesus encouraged it. He once told the disciples a parable about a persistent widow to urge them to keep praying (Luke 18:1–8). The widow needed justice, so she pleaded her case to a certain judge over and over. The judge was not a godly man and repeatedly refused to help the widow. Eventually, though, he gave the widow what she wanted to stop her from bothering him. Jesus' point? If this ungodly man would respond favorably to spare himself, God will most certainly answer the ones He loves. "God will always give what is right to his people who cry to him night and day, and he will not be slow to answer them," Jesus said. "I tell you, God will help his people quickly" (Luke 18:7–8 NCV). Again Jesus promised, "Everyone who asks receives, and the one who seeks finds, and to the one who knocks it will be opened. . . . If you then, who are evil, know how to give good gifts to your children, how much more will your Father who is in heaven give good things to those who ask him!" (Matthew 7:8, 11). God wants us to approach Him with our needs. And it's okay to be persistent, like the blind beggar along the road outside Jericho who called out to Jesus for mercy. Even though the crowds rebuked him, he called out the same words again, and Jesus responded, restoring his sight. Or like the Canaanite woman who sought healing for her daughter. At first Jesus remained silent; then He turned her down. But the woman asked again. This time Jesus answered, "O woman, great is your faith! Be it done for you as you desire" (Matthew 15:28).

Go ahead. Ask Him one more time.

*Father, thank You for listening to my every request.*
*Even in the asking, You are building my faith.*
*So I'll keep asking. Amen.*

# Die to Live

*"Whoever finds his life will lose it, and whoever loses his life for my sake will find it."*

MATTHEW 10:39

ose your life to find it. *Shouldn't that be the other way around?* But Jesus' statement in Matthew is just one example of the Bible's sometimes backward-sounding logic. Truth is, without the Holy Spirit's help, much of God's Word doesn't make a whole lot of sense. A. W. Tozer wrote:

> *A real Christian is an odd number anyway. He feels supreme love for One whom he has never seen, talks familiarly every day to Someone he cannot see, expects to go to heaven on the virtue of Another, empties himself in order to be full, admits he is wrong so he can be declared right, goes down in order to get up, is strongest when he is weakest, richest when he is poorest and happiest when he feels worst. He dies so he can live, forsakes in order to have, gives away so he can keep, sees the invisible, hears the inaudible and knows that which passeth knowledge.\**

So what does Jesus mean when He tells us that by losing

our lives for His sake we will find them? His meaning is twofold. For some of Jesus' followers, professing faith in Him will lead to losing their lives literally—they will be martyred for their faith. For every believer, though, true faith in Christ involves dying to self to live for Christ (Galatians 2:20). It involves letting go of self to grab hold of Christ alone. Jesus said, "If anyone would come after me, let him deny himself and take up his cross and follow me" (Matthew 16:24). Taking up one's cross—living completely surrendered to God—echoes the complete sacrifice that Christ made for us on the cross. But Christ's sacrifice also brought life, and so does ours. When we choose Christ over self, when we forsake the world to follow Him, we gain abundant life now and eternal life to come. "Most assuredly," said Jesus, "unless a grain of wheat falls into the ground and dies, it remains alone; but if it dies, it produces much grain. He who loves his life will lose it, and he who hates his life in this world will keep it for eternal life. . .and where I am, there My servant will be also. If anyone serves Me, him My Father will honor" (John 12:24–26 NKJV).

*Lord, You've given me true life through the cross—life for my soul now and in eternity. Every day, show me more of what it means to lose my life for You. Amen.*

---

*A. W. Tozer, The Root of Righteousness (Chicago: Moody Publishers, 2015), 189.

# "Shepherd Me!"

*The LORD is my shepherd. . . . Yea, though I walk through the valley of the shadow of death, I will fear no evil: for thou art with me; thy rod and thy staff they comfort me.*
PSALM 23:1, 4 KJV

A t age five it was the dark. At age nine it was spiders. At age sixteen it was her driver's license test (and spiders). At age twenty-seven it was finances. At age thirty-four it was a health scare. At age. . . No matter what our age, it seems fear is always with us. Yet no matter what we're afraid of, we always have a reason *not* to fear.

In his well-known psalm, Psalm 23, David identified God with an image that appears throughout scripture: the Lord as shepherd. Both Old and New Testament writers referred to God's guiding presence in believers' lives in terms of shepherding. For David, the Lord as his shepherd meant that even in the most frightening times—"the valley of the shadow of death"—he would not fear because God was with him. Like a shepherd fending off predators and gently leading the sheep with the tools of his trade, God was there, guarding and guiding David.

Without a shepherd, a sheep's life is hazardous. There are thickets and ditches that trap and wolves that devour. Sound familiar? Life is full of fears, the most threatening being death. But we believers have a shepherd and savior from our fears. Jesus said, "If anyone enters by me, he will be saved and will go in and out and find pasture. The thief comes only to steal and kill and destroy. I came that they may have life and have it abundantly. . . . I am the good shepherd. I know my own and my own know me. . .and I lay down my life for the sheep" (John 10:9–10, 14–15). Such a promise is reason enough not to fear.

Each of us as a believer is one of the Lord's flock. He knows us individually, calling us by name, and cares for us beyond anything we could imagine. He is our Good Shepherd, and we will not fear even the valleys because He is with us—guarding and guiding, shepherding us through life. "Now may the God of peace who brought again from the dead our Lord Jesus, the great shepherd of the sheep, by the blood of the eternal covenant, equip you with everything good that you may do his will, working in us that which is pleasing in his sight" (Hebrews 13:20–21).

*Lord, when I face my fears, please remind me that I don't face them alone. You, my Good Shepherd, walk before me. Amen.*

# A Lesson in Humility

*Humble yourselves, therefore, under the mighty hand of God so that at the proper time he may exalt you.*
1 PETER 5:6

The last months had been no picnic. She still believed she was where God wanted her to be, but the joy of following had led to a place of hardship. Sometimes she wished she could go back, plug her ears, and pretend she didn't hear God. Sometimes she desperately wanted to look for an escape route. Sometimes she was tempted to shake her fist at God and cry out, "Why? Why have You brought me here to suffer?" One thing she was sure of: God was working in her life.

God is continually working in our lives, using every moment to fulfill His plans. And He will fulfill them. "Have you not heard that I determined it long ago?" the Lord asked. "I planned from days of old what now I bring to pass" (2 Kings 19:25). When we're swimming in blessings, we cheer at those words. But what if God's plan involves molding us through hardship? What if His doing something better requires some bitterness along the way? Do we push against His mighty hand? Or do we humble ourselves and wait for Him to work?

Jesus knew what it meant to humble Himself. He left His throne in heaven to wash the feet of sinners. He tasted the bitterness of death for our sake. And His mentality is to be our own. Paul instructed believers in Philippi, "Have this mind among yourselves, which is yours in Christ Jesus, who, though he was in the form of God, did not count equality with God a thing to be grasped, but emptied himself, by taking the form of a servant, being born in the likeness of men. And being found in human form, he humbled himself by becoming obedient to the point of death, even death on a cross" (Philippians 2:5–8). The Son submitted to the Father. He made Himself low—until God lifted Him up. Paul continued, "Therefore God has highly exalted him and bestowed on him the name that is above every name" (Philippians 2:9).

God is continually working in your life. When in His sovereignty He brings you through challenging times, don't resist His mighty hand—He's using even the rough moments for your good and His glory. Instead, "give your[self] completely to God. . . . Humble yourself in the Lord's presence." And in due time "he will honor you" (James 4:7, 10 NCV).

*God, I don't like where I am right now, but I won't fight what You're doing in my life. I choose to humble myself before You so that You can lift me up. Amen.*

# Relax—It's the Sabbath

*Jesus said to them, "The Sabbath was made for man,
and not man for the Sabbath. So the Son of
Man is Lord even of the Sabbath."*
MARK 2:27–28 NASB

Sabbath. Sunday. The day of rest. We call it different names, and our opinions on it vary. Is it a day like any other, a catchall for the loose ends of the week, or a chance to catch up on some z's? Do we hit PAUSE on everything but worship and reflection? Our view on the Sabbath may be a jumble of tradition, practicality, and scripture. It may even become a source of tension. What are we supposed to do about the Sabbath?

The Pharisees, of course, had rules for the Sabbath, and one Sabbath, Jesus' disciples broke those rules. As they were traveling through a grain field, the disciples, who were hungry, began to pick off some heads of grain to eat. When the Pharisees pointed out this infraction, Jesus replied:

> *"Have you not read what David did when he
> was hungry, and those who were with him: how
> he entered the house of God and ate the bread
> of the Presence, which it was not lawful for him
> to eat nor for those who were with him, but only
> for the priests? Or have you not read in the Law
> how on the Sabbath the priests in the temple*

*profane the Sabbath and are guiltless? I tell*
*you, something greater than the temple is here.*
*And if you had known what this means, 'I desire*
*mercy, and not sacrifice,' you would not have*
*condemned the guiltless."* (Matthew 12:3–7)

While the Pharisees were shortsighted amid all their rules and the regulations they thought they knew, Jesus was looking toward "something greater." His death on the cross would bring the kind of rest that the Sabbath only represented—a rest for the soul from the toils of living up to the law (Matthew 11:28). Of Jesus' offered rest, John MacArthur wrote, "It was an offer of an abiding Sabbath rest. He was the fulfillment of all that the Sabbaths pictured. And we don't need the picture if we have the reality."* Christ offered freedom from the regulations; He offered rest. After Christ, the Sabbath became what it was intended to be—a blessing, not a burden.

A final thought: God rested on the seventh day (Genesis 2:3). No regulation bound Him, but He set the pace for us. Will you join Him in some rest this Sabbath?

*God, thank You for rest—rest for my body each*
*week and rest for my soul in eternity. Amen.*

---

*John MacArthur, *Worship: The Ultimate Priority*
(Chicago: Moody Publishers, 2012), 132.

## "For God So Loved"

*For God so loved the world, that he gave his only begotten Son, that whosoever believeth in him should not perish, but have everlasting life.*

JOHN 3:16 KJV

You might be familiar with the children's book *Guess How Much I Love You.** It's the story of Little Nutbrown Hare and his father, Big Nutbrown Hare. Throughout the pages, Little Nutbrown Hare tries to show his father how much he loves him—as wide as his arms can stretch and as high as he can reach, up to the height of his hops and way out to the moon. But each time, the father shows he loves much more—as wide as *his* arms can stretch. . .way out to the moon and back.

John 3:16 is one of the most well-known verses in the Bible, and for good reason. Using only about two dozen words, John encapsulated the Gospel message. "For God so loved the world, that he gave his only begotten Son, that whosoever believeth in him should not perish, but have everlasting life" (KJV). God so loved us that He sent His Son to save us. By believing in Him, we have eternal life. What love! But what makes that love even greater is the fact that God loved us when we were unlovable. Paul explained, "For while we were still weak, at the right time Christ died for the ungodly. For one will scarcely die for a righteous person—though perhaps for a good person one would dare even to die—but God shows his love for us in that while we were still sinners, Christ died for us" (Romans 5:6–8). We had nothing to offer in our sinful state—not even our love. "We love because he *first* loved us," John wrote (1 John 4:19, emphasis added). And God so loved us.

The heavenly Father's love is indeed vast. And its extent is something God is forever revealing to our hearts. Paul's prayer for the Ephesians was "that according to the riches of his glory he may grant you to be strengthened with power through his Spirit in your inner being, so that Christ may dwell in your hearts through faith—that you, being rooted and grounded in love, may have strength to comprehend with all the saints what is the breadth and length and height and depth, and to know the love of Christ that surpasses knowledge" (Ephesians 3:16–19). How much does God love us? As wide as Christ's outstretched arms on the cross. From heaven to earth and back.

*Father, I love You so much. Thank You for the reminder that You love me much more. Amen.*

*Sam McBratney, *Guess How Much I Love You* (Somerville, MA: Candlewick, 2008).

## Like Sponges

*And do not be conformed to this world, but be transformed*
*by the renewing of your mind, so that you may prove*
*what the will of God is, that which is good*
*and acceptable and perfect.*
ROMANS 12:2 NASB

Sponges are curious things. Place one on a wet counter and it slurps the liquid, swelling in size and darkening in color. Whatever it soaks up transforms it. We say children are like sponges because their minds soak up everything around them. Whatever they hear and see transforms them. And the same is true of our grown-up minds. Whatever we fill our heads with transforms us.

A changed mind is at the core of salvation. When we believe in Jesus, God changes who we are, beginning with how we think—our beliefs, our moral compass, and so on. Our former ways no longer characterize us—they belong to minds that have not yet been enlightened by God's truth. Paul told believers, "You must no longer walk as the Gentiles do, in the futility of their minds. They are darkened in their understanding, alienated from the life of God because of the ignorance that is in them, due to their hardness of heart. . . . But that is not the way you learned Christ!—assuming that you have heard about him and were taught in him, as the truth is in Jesus, to put off your old self, which belongs to your former manner of life and is corrupt. . .and to be renewed in the spirit of your minds" (Ephesians 4:17–18, 20–23). New mind intact, a believer starts life as a Christian with a new nature (verse 24), and rather than being "conformed to this world," she is to live out her new nature by being transformed daily.

What fuels this daily transformation? The renewing of the mind. So how do we renew our minds?

First, we need to ask for help. The renewal that the Bible speaks about comes only through the Holy Spirit. On our own we cannot understand godly things, but with the Spirit abiding in us, we can understand even the thoughts of our Lord (1 Corinthians 2:16).

Then we need to think deeply on God's Word, letting it "dwell" in us "richly" (Colossians 3:16). Philippians 4:8 (NKJV) tells us, "Whatever things are true, whatever things are noble, whatever things are just, whatever things are pure, whatever things are lovely. . .meditate on these things." As we fill our minds with scripture, we're filled with life-changing words. As we soak up His Word, it transforms us.

*Holy Spirit, renew my mind through the Word.*
*I want to be so soaked in scripture that my every*
*thought and action is transformed. Amen.*

# Doubtless

*Thomas answered him, "My Lord and my God!" Jesus said to him, "Have you believed because you have seen me? Blessed are those who have not seen and yet have believed."*
JOHN 20:28–29

H e's known as doubting Thomas. The resurrected Lord had appeared to the disciples and showed them His nail-scarred hands and side. But Thomas wasn't there, so the disciples had to relay what they'd seen. Upon hearing the incredible news, Thomas was doubtful; he needed proof. Unless he saw and touched the marks on Jesus' hands and side himself, he would not believe.

Thomas wasn't the first believer to have doubts. When God told Moses that He was sending him to free Israel, Moses doubted his own ability. "Who am I," he asked, "that I should go to Pharaoh and bring the children of Israel out of Egypt?" (Exodus 3:11). John the Baptist was imprisoned when he heard reports about "the deeds of the Christ" (Matthew 11:2). In response, he sent a message to Jesus: "Are you the one who is to come, or shall we look for another?" (Matthew 11:3). And Philip—right after Jesus' declaration that He is the way, the truth, and the life and that through Him we know God (John 14:6–7)—requested a bit more evidence: "Lord, show us the Father, and it is enough for us" (John 14:8).

How did God react to the doubters? Out of His love He supplied exactly what each one needed to believe. For Moses, it was reassurance—"I will be with you, and this shall be the sign for you, that I have sent you" (Exodus 3:12). For John, it was confirmation—"Go and tell John what you hear and see: the blind receive their sight and the lame walk, lepers are cleansed and the deaf hear, and the dead are raised up" (Matthew 11:4–5). For Philip, it was the facts—"Have I been with you so long, and you still do not know me, Philip? . . . Believe me. . .or else believe on account of the works themselves" (John 14:9, 11).

And for Thomas, it was physical proof. A week and a day later, Jesus appeared again. To Thomas, in an echo of Thomas's words, He said, "Put your finger here, and see my hands; and put out your hand, and place it in my side. Do not disbelieve, but believe" (John 20:27).

God knows that believing is difficult, especially without sight. "Blessed are those who have not seen and yet have believed," Jesus said (John 20:29). And when we cry out to Him, "I believe; help my unbelief!" (Mark 9:24), He will reach out to us, no doubt about it.

*God, I believe in You. Help me shed my doubts. Amen.*

# Contented

*Be content with what you have, for he has said,*
*"I will never leave you nor forsake you."*
HEBREWS 13:5

❧

H ow much is enough? Considering the overabundance that's out there—from row upon row of vehicles at dealerships to crammed store aisles to the ever-present next-best in devices—it's a question we ought to ask ourselves. There's *so much stuff* our hearts can pine after that the pining can go on and on. No sooner do we get one thing than something else catches our eye, and that something will be enough, surely! But it isn't. Renowned preacher Charles Spurgeon once said, "You say, 'If I had a little more, I should be very satisfied.' You make a mistake. If you are not content with what you have, you would not be satisfied if it were doubled." Solomon too understood the futility of trying to reach a place of satisfaction in the pursuit of more. He shared this piece of wisdom with readers: "It is better to be content with what little you have. Otherwise, you will always be struggling for more, and that is like chasing the wind" (Ecclesiastes 4:6 NCV).

It may or may not be a surprise, but the Bible's definition of enough is radically different from the Western world's definition, where every billboard, commercial, and online ad touts that enough is more. Christians should be able to find satisfaction in the bare necessities. Paul wrote to Timothy, "Now godliness with contentment is great gain. For we brought nothing into this world, and it is certain we can carry nothing out. And having food and clothing, with these we shall be content" (1 Timothy 6:6–8 NKJV). *So a shirt on your back and a meal in your belly is enough? How?*

The kind of contentment Paul wrote about has nothing to do with how much or how little a person owns but everything to do with the One who satisfies. In a passage on God's provision, Paul told believers, "I have learned in whatever state I am, to be content: I know how to be abased, and I know how to abound. Everywhere and in all things I have learned both to be full and to be hungry, both to abound and to suffer need. I can do all things through Christ who strengthens me" (Philippians 4:11–13 NKJV). Paul could be content trusting in God's presence to get him through times of plenty and need. He could be content resting in the God who met his deepest longings. He could be content knowing that what God gave was enough.

*God, where You are, no matter what else fills my life,*
*I will be content. And You are always with me. Amen.*

# All Ready?

*"Therefore you also must be ready, for the Son of Man is coming at an hour you do not expect."*

MATTHEW 24:44

Today could be the day. Christ has promised to return, and He will, any moment now. But somehow in the midst of our day-to-day, the certainty—the immediacy—of Christ's return is sometimes the last thing on our minds.

Knowing us only too well, Jesus cautioned believers to remain alert, to keep the thought of His second coming at the forefront of our minds. He compared the waiting period that would end with His arrival to the time leading up to the flood: "But as the days of Noah were, so also will the coming of the Son of Man be. For as in the days before the flood, they were eating and drinking, marrying and giving in marriage, until the day that Noah entered the ark, and did not know until the flood came and took them all away, so also will the coming of the Son of Man be" (Matthew 24:37–39 NKJV). While the people were caught up in life's daily concerns, the flood came and caught them unawares. This wouldn't be the case for believers who were watching and waiting for Christ to come. Though they could not predict the hour, they could prepare. Jesus said, "Be dressed, ready for service, and have your lamps shining. Be like servants who are waiting for their master to come home from a wedding party. When he comes and knocks, the servants immediately open the door for him. . . . Those servants will be blessed when he comes in and finds them still waiting, even if it is midnight or later" (Luke 12:35–36, 38 NCV).

Peter continued Jesus' themes of watchfulness and readiness at all times, no matter how lengthy the wait. He reminded believers not to be lulled by scoffers into thinking that because the world is humming along as it always has, it always will (2 Peter 3:4). Believers know better. Christ will return, and God will judge: "The day of the Lord will come like a thief. . .and the earth and the works that are done on it will be exposed" (2 Peter 3:10). And since we know what's ahead, "what sort of people ought [we] to be in lives of holiness and godliness, waiting for and hastening the coming of the day of God" (2 Peter 3:11–12)! Let's watch for Him. Let's use this time to get ready, to live every day in anticipation. Today could be the day.

*Lord, I've been so preoccupied with living that I haven't thought about You coming back. I'm sorry. When You return, help me to be ready and waiting. Amen.*

# Holy Pruning

*This is my prayer for you. . .that you will be filled with*
*the good things produced in your life by Christ*
*to bring glory and praise to God.*
PHILIPPIANS 1:9, 11 NCV

God's first recorded order for man was "Be fruitful and multiply" (Genesis 1:28). Christians today are to be fruitful too, but not just in populating the earth. In Romans we're told that when God releases us from the bondage of the law, He does it "so that [we] may belong to another, to him who has been raised from the dead, in order that we may bear fruit for God" (Romans 7:4). And in the book of John, Jesus explained to His disciples and, by extension, to all believers that He handpicked us with plans for us to bear fruit: "You did not choose me, but I chose you and appointed you that you should go and bear fruit and that your fruit should abide" (John 15:16). God's orders? Be fruitful! Yield spiritual fruit—what the New Testament defines as godly attitudes, righteous behavior, praise, and the leading of nonbelievers to faith*—and the more, the better. "By this my Father is glorified," Jesus said, "that you bear *much* fruit" (John 15:8, emphasis added).

If the prospect of bearing an abundance of fruit is overwhelming, keep this in mind: it is through God that we bear fruit at all, and He is working in us to make us more fruitful. In one of the Bible's beautiful metaphors of Christianity, Jesus becomes the vine, the Father the vinedresser, and believers the branches:

*"I am the true vine, and My Father is the vinedresser. Every branch in Me that does not bear fruit He takes away; and every branch that bears fruit He prunes, that it may bear more fruit. You are already clean because of the word which I have spoken to you. Abide in Me, and I in you. As the branch cannot bear fruit of itself, unless it abides in the vine, neither can you, unless you abide in Me.*

*"I am the vine, you are the branches. He who abides in Me, and I in him, bears much fruit; for without Me you can do nothing."*
(John 15:1–5 NKJV)

As we abide in the vine, drawing life from Him, God is pruning, cutting away anything in our lives that impedes our growth, lopping off a sin here and trimming back a bad habit there. God's pruning isn't pleasant, but it will make the branches flourish (Hebrews 12:11).

*Father, I can feel Your pruning in my life, and Your shears hurt. But I've seen You work before, and it always yields fruit. Amen.*

---

*John MacArthur, *The MacArthur Bible Commentary* (Nashville: Thomas Nelson, 2005), 1407.

# Making Everything Beautiful

*It is not fancy hair, gold jewelry, or fine clothes that should make you beautiful. No, your beauty should come from within you—the beauty of a gentle and quiet spirit that will never be destroyed and is very precious to God.*

1 PETER 3:3–4 NCV

W hatever you look like on the outside, odds are there's *something* you would change. Next time you're standing face-to-face with yourself at the mirror, try this: see your appearance not as a result of happenstance, genes mixing with genes, but as the workmanship of the Creator. Of God the psalmist wrote, "You made my whole being; you formed me in my mother's body. I praise you because you made me in an amazing and wonderful way. What you have done is wonderful. I know this very well" (Psalm 139:13–14 NCV). From start to finish, head to toe, God designed you—with care and intention, in an amazing and wonderful way.

Why is it, then, that we so often question our Maker? "Woe to him who strives with him who formed him, a pot among earthen pots!" the Lord said. "Does the clay say to him who forms it, 'What are you making?' or 'Your work has no handles'?" (Isaiah 45:9). Yet we, the creation, look at what the Creator has made and find things we would have done differently. We overlook the truth that when God creates—just as when He plans—He does so with perfection. And He does so with purpose.

That purpose goes deeper than skin and bones. God is most concerned with what's inside. When the Lord sent Samuel to anoint the next king of Israel, the young shepherd David, He told Samuel, "Do not look on his appearance or on the height of his stature. . . . For the LORD sees not as man sees: man looks on the outward appearance, but the LORD looks on the heart" (1 Samuel 16:7). It didn't matter if David was impressive physically; God was peering inside, to his heart. He's still gazing on our hearts, and if our focus is the outer shell, we'll miss it. While we expend a good deal of energy on the surface, trying to make the outer shell more beautiful, God is working within. He is making us beautiful in ways that won't become clear and won't be complete until heaven. Now if only we would begin to see as God sees. If only we would appreciate the beauty God creates in us, standing face-to-face with ourselves at the mirror!

*God, when I pick apart what You've created, give me eyes to*
*see as You do. I'm beautiful to You—outside and in—*
*and I'll become more beautiful still. Amen.*

# Why We Love

*We love because he first loved us.*
1 John 4:19

aybe he sat off to the side. Maybe he was hovering around the fringes of the group or standing right in the middle. But after hearing Jesus' expert reply to the Sadducees, the scribe asked his own question. "Which commandment is the most important of all?" (Mark 12:28). Jesus' answer has become the backbone of Christian life: love God with everything in you, and love your neighbor as yourself (Mark 12:29–31). Put simply, love is huge. Paul even wrote that "the whole law is fulfilled in one word: 'You shall love your neighbor as yourself'" (Galatians 5:14; see also Romans 13:9).

Why is love so paramount? Because God Himself is love (1 John 4:8, 16). It is through Him that we know love ourselves. God put an exclamation point on His love at the cross. "In this the love of God was made manifest among us, that God sent his only Son into the world, so that we might live through him. In this is love, not that we have loved God but that he loved us and sent his Son to be the propitiation for our sins" (1 John 4:9–10). God did the loving, and now we respond to His love with love. John continued, "Beloved, if God so loved us, we also ought to love one another" (1 John 4:11).

That's all well and good, but what if your neighbor—whether next door or an ocean away—is someone you don't particularly like? How do you love when your heart isn't in it? Author C. S. Lewis had this to say: "The rule for all of us is perfectly simple. Do not waste time bothering whether you 'love' your neighbour; act as if you did. As soon as we do this we find one of the great secrets. When you are behaving as if you loved someone, you will presently come to love him."* While this "fake it till you make it" version of love may seem to lack feeling, that is precisely the point according to Lewis, because "Christian Love, either towards God or towards man, is an affair of the will." Once we choose to love, God will work in our hearts. "He will give us feelings of love if He pleases," Lewis concluded.† We are forever directed back to Love itself. God loved us, so we love. We love through God in us.

*God, I try so hard to love others. But it's because of Your love that I choose to love, and it's because of Your presence that I can love. Help me to love like You do. Amen.*

---

*C. S. Lewis, *Mere Christianity* (New York: HarperCollins, 2001), 131.
†Ibid., 132.

# "I Don't Get It"

*Think over what I say, for the Lord will give you understanding in everything.*

2 TIMOTHY 2:7

~

The girl sat at the kitchen table—head in her hands, frown on her face. She'd been staring at the numbers scribbled on the notebook paper in front of her for many minutes now. Had she finally solved the problem? Yes, she had! Still locked in her thoughts, she heard the scrape of chair legs beside her. Her father sat down at the kitchen table—head next to hers, love across his face—and scanned the page. Then he tapped his finger on a decimal point. Click, click went the gears in her brain. . . Ah! Now she understood.

Each day of our Christian lives we are maturing, growing spiritually. In the process, sometimes we don't understand; sometimes we don't even realize we're mistaken. What's a girl to do? Rely on God—to point out our failings and flaws and to point us toward understanding.

On one journey during Jesus' earthly ministry, the disciples had not remembered to bring bread. Using the moment to share deeper wisdom, Jesus told them, "Watch and beware of the leaven of the Pharisees and Sadducees" (Matthew 16:6). Now, the disciples were intelligent men, but this time they missed the point. They were so concerned about the physical bread they lacked, they both forgot the ability of the One who stood before them and failed to hear His words. Jesus confronted them with what they really lacked—faith and understanding—and reiterated His lesson: "O you of little faith, why do you reason among yourselves because you have brought no bread? Do you not yet understand, or remember the five loaves of the five thousand and how many baskets you took up? . . . How is it you do not understand that I did not speak to you concerning bread?—but to beware of the leaven of the Pharisees and Sadducees" (Matthew 16:8–9, 11 NKJV). The Bible tells us they *then* understood what Jesus meant (Matthew 16:12). With some help, they got it.

Believers are never without help when we need it. After Jesus' ascension to heaven, the Holy Spirit came to aid us in understanding the things of God. Jesus said, "The Helper. . .will teach you all things" (John 14:26). And again, "When he, the Spirit of truth, is come, he will guide you into all truth" (John 16:13 KJV). Each day we put one foot in front of the other; we do our best to make sense of holy things, knowing that God is beside us, helping us understand.

*Holy Spirit, show me where I'm not getting it.*
*I want to understand. Amen.*

# Step 2: Do

*But the one who looks into the perfect law, the law of liberty, and perseveres, being no hearer who forgets but a doer who acts, he will be blessed in his doing.*

JAMES 1:25

❧

Take one pill daily. Watch your step. Ferry departs at 10:00 a.m. Read through instructions before beginning. Detour ahead. . . Every day we have a choice—to heed direction or pay no attention to it. Most times, what we're told is for our benefit. Let your medicine gather dust and you won't get any better. Don't look where you're going and you could face-plant. Show up late and you'll miss the boat. Plunge right in and you risk more work. Drive by that detour sign and you might find yourself at a dead end.

God's Word is full of direction too, and it's always beneficial. It tells us how to find life through the Savior, and then how to live life in Him. But we shouldn't stop at the first step of hearing. We have to *follow* what the Bible says if we want to reap the benefits. Jesus told the multitudes, "Why do you call me 'Lord, Lord,' and not do what I tell you? Everyone who comes to me and hears my words and does them, I will show you what he is like: he is like a man building a house, who dug deep and laid the foundation on the rock. And when a flood arose, the stream broke against that house and could not shake it, because it had been well built" (Luke 6:46–48). Building our lives on true faith, which leads to obedience, is the only way to gain future security and present peace of mind.

James picked up Jesus' message in a letter to dispersed believers. He wrote, "Do what God's teaching says; when you only listen and do nothing, you are fooling yourselves. Those who hear God's teaching and do nothing are like people who look at themselves in a mirror. They see their faces and then go away and quickly forget what they looked like. But the truly happy people are those who carefully study God's perfect law that makes people free, and they continue to study it. They do not forget what they heard, but they obey what God's teaching says. Those who do this will be made happy" (James 1:22–25 NCV). Did you catch that last part? The hearer who obeys "will be *made* happy." God honors obedience. He blesses those who choose to heed His direction.

So let's read, then do. We will be blessed in the doing.

*God, the Bible is not meant for me to glance over and then forget. Its words bring life. Through Your Spirit, help me hear and obey. Amen.*

# All-Out Pursuit

*"You will seek me and find me,*
*when you seek me with all your heart."*
JEREMIAH 29:13

*n*umber seven of seven, the letter to the church in Laodicea got straight to the point and did not mince words: " 'I [the Amen] know your deeds, that you are neither cold nor hot; I wish that you were cold or hot. So because you are lukewarm, and neither hot nor cold, I will spit you out of My mouth' " (Revelation 3:15–16 NASB). The Laodiceans had not given Christ the cold shoulder, yet neither had they warmly embraced Him. They claimed to believe, yet their actions were still lukewarm and, as such, were repulsive to Christ.

While it was hypocritical faith that defined the Laodicean church and caused Christ's displeasure, even sincere believers can be "lukewarm" in their faith. But nowhere does the Bible praise tepidness. So immense was God's sacrifice, so complete was His mercy, that believers owe Him more than "half-hearted" in return. He deserves total devotion—an all-out pursuit.

The Bible's very language reflects the zeal that should define a life lived for God. Paul considered everything else garbage when compared to knowing Christ and becoming Christlike; his passion was "forgetting what lies behind and *straining forward* to what lies ahead" (Philippians 3:13, emphasis added). Paul urged Timothy not to let his faithfulness in serving God become an ember; rather,

Timothy should "*fan into flame* the gift of God" (2 Timothy 1:6, emphasis added). Jesus quoted the greatest commandment as "You shall love the Lord your God with *all* your heart and with *all* your soul and with *all* your mind and with *all* your strength" (Mark 12:30, emphasis added). And David declared, "My soul *followeth hard* after thee" (Psalm 63:8 KJV, emphasis added).

Believers are to run, not stroll, toward God. We should follow after Him and His ways with a greater intensity than we do anything else. In his classic work *The Pursuit of God*, A. W. Tozer wrote, "I want deliberately to encourage this mighty longing after God. . . . Complacency is a deadly foe of all spiritual growth. Acute desire must be present or there will be no manifestation of Christ to His people. He waits to be wanted."*

God is waiting. And "He is a rewarder of those who diligently seek Him" (Hebrews 11:6 NKJV). Are you ready to go all out?

*God, I haven't been pursuing You like I should. Forgive me. Please show me where my faith life is lukewarm and increase my fervor. I sense You even now, calling me, urging me to pursue You like never before. Amen.*

---

*A. W. Tozer, *The Pursuit of God* (Chicago: Moody Publishers, 2015), 23.

## Keep Up the Good Work

*And let us not grow weary of doing good, for in due*
*season we will reap, if we do not give up.*
GALATIANS 6:9

~

With a sigh, she sank into bed. Another day had passed. Another day of trying to do what was right in a world that did so much wrong. Another day of fighting the good fight when she seemed to lose more battles than she won. Another day had passed, and she was weary—muscles and soul.

The longer we're Christians, the likelier we are to know what it means to grow weary. On this earth of ours, cheaters do prosper, and sometimes the good work only makes a dent in the bad. It's not our imagination—Jesus affirmed there would be troubles in this life, while Paul declared that "the days are evil" (Ephesians 5:16)—but doing good is not a lost cause. With His bad tidings, Jesus brought hope. "Take heart; I have overcome the world," He said (John 16:33). And Paul encouraged believers to "[make] the best use of the time" (Ephesians 5:16). For now God's goodwill extends to everyone: the Father "causes His sun to rise on the evil and the good, and sends rain on the righteous and the unrighteous" (Matthew 5:45 NASB). For now God is patiently bearing evil so that His chosen make their way to Him (2 Peter 3:9). But His forbearance won't go on forever.

So for now, believers are not to worry when evil seems to have the advantage; rather, they are to rest in the sovereignty of God, who reigns over the darkness and will make all things right. David wrote of God's saints, "Fret not yourself because of evildoers; be not envious of wrongdoers! For they will soon fade like the grass and wither like the green herb. Trust in the Lord, and do good; dwell in the land and befriend faithfulness. . . . He will bring forth your righteousness as the light, and your justice as the noonday" (Psalm 37:1–3, 6).

And for now, believers are not to grow weary of doing good. Paul told the church in Corinth, "Do not let anything move you. Always give yourselves fully to the work of the Lord, because you know that your work in the Lord is never wasted" (1 Corinthians 15:58 NCV). Whatever we do for God has value. Even at the end of days when the good we do seems to be all for nothing, we have reason to call on our Strength and keep up the good work.

*God, energize me to do the good things You've prepared for me. Doing good is never in vain—You will use Your people's good works for Your glory and reward them in heaven. Amen.*

# "I'll Pray for You"

*If God be for us, who can be against us? . . . It is Christ that died, yea rather, that is risen again, who is even at the right hand of God, who also maketh intercession for us.*

ROMANS 8:31, 34 KJV

When we're tossed by life's events and burdened by its demands, is anything so sweet as hearing the words "I'll pray for you"? Intercession for a fellow believer is a precious gift. It's not what's left at the bottom of the barrel but rather is access to an all-loving, all-powerful Father. Prayers are potent things (James 5:16). And if the petitions of our brothers and sisters in Christ have power, how much more so do our Lord's?

Christ's ministry did not end the moment He left this earth. The Bible tells us that He continues to minister to believers from His heavenly throne, interceding to God on our behalf. Hebrews says of the One who is powerful enough to redeem us "to the uttermost," "he always lives to make intercession for [us]" (7:25). Yet Jesus prayed for believers before He returned to heaven. What did He request of His Father? He prayed for God's presence, nature, and love to indwell believers. He prayed that God would be with us now and that we would be with Him in eternity. Spend some time soaking in His words. No prayer is so sweet:

> *"I do not ask for these only, but also for those who will believe in me through their word,*

*that they may all be one, just as you, Father, are in me, and I in you, that they also may be in us, so that the world may believe that you have sent me. The glory that you have given me I have given to them, that they may be one even as we are one, I in them and you in me, that they may become perfectly one, so that the world may know that you sent me and loved them even as you loved me. Father, I desire that they also, whom you have given me, may be with me where I am, to see my glory that you have given me because you loved me before the foundation of the world. O righteous Father, even though the world does not know you, I know you, and these know that you have sent me. I made known to them your name, and I will continue to make it known, that the love with which you have loved me may be in them, and I in them."*
(John 17:20–26)

*Lord, thank You for Your prayers. What joy and peace I feel in knowing that You are with me, that You are praying for me! Amen.*

# First Things First

*Delight yourself in the LORD, and he will*
*give you the desires of your heart.*
PSALM 37:4

She couldn't—shouldn't—complain. Her life was full of bless-ings. But there was still that one thing. The one missing piece she wanted more than anything. If only it were hers, she would have all her heart desired.

What is it you want? What's the missing piece (or pieces) in your life that you would give anything to grasp? It could be landing your dream job or getting married or starting a family or achieving a long-held goal. Whatever it is, here's some advice rooted in biblical wisdom: don't put the cart before the horse.

To understand, take a couple of steps back. As part of His Sermon on the Mount, Jesus addressed the topic of anxiety. Recognizing that daily cares like food and clothing often con-sumed the crowd's thoughts, Jesus counseled His audience to think deeper and get their priorities sorted. "Is not life more than food, and the body more than clothing?" He asked them (Matthew 6:25). The Creator of all things knew that being well fed and well dressed would do nothing for a deprived soul. In their minds, then, spiritual concerns needed to take precedence over physical ones: "Therefore do not be anxious, saying, 'What shall we eat?' or 'What shall we drink?' or 'What shall we wear?' For the Gentiles seek after all these things, and your heavenly

Father knows that you need them all. But *seek first* the kingdom of God and his righteousness, and all these things will be added to you" (Matthew 6:31–33, emphasis added). In other words, concern yourself with soul issues first, and God will take care of the rest. A soul relying on God for eternal provision can also rely on Him for earthly care (Romans 8:32).

"Seek first the kingdom of God. . .and all these things will be added to you." We see the same pattern throughout the Bible. "Humble yourselves before the Lord, and he will exalt you" (James 4:10). "Commit your works to the LORD and your plans will be established" (Proverbs 16:3 NASB). "Delight yourself in the LORD, and he will give you the desires of your heart (Psalm 37:4). Whatever our hopes, dreams, or wishes, the pursuit of them must come second to God in our hearts. And when we put Him first, we discover a miraculous truth: He meets our every need and our every desire.

*God, You know my heart's desire, what I long for. Even if it*
*materialized this very moment, it wouldn't be enough.*
*But with You filling my heart to the brim,*
*everything else falls into place. Amen.*

# Foiled?

*The LORD of hosts has sworn: "As I have planned,*
*so shall it be, and as I have purposed, so shall it stand."*
ISAIAH 14:24

Do you recognize any of these thoughts? *What if I pick a path that isn't God's will for my life? What if by choosing "this" over "that" I won't be where God wants me? What if I've done something to stop God from working? What if I've missed out on God's best for me?* Whether you're agonizing over a decision you've yet to make or you're worrying over one you've already made, you might wonder if you can mess up the plans God has for you. But the Bible is clear-cut here: we cannot foil God.

Among almighty God's many attributes are His omniscience, omnipotence, and sovereignty. He knows all, controls all, and rules all; therefore, He is fully capable of bringing all His plans to pass. The psalmist declared, "He determines the number of the stars. . . . Great is our Lord, and abundant in power; his understanding is beyond measure" (Psalm 147:4–5), and "The counsel of the LORD stands forever, the plans of His heart from generation to generation" (Psalm 33:11 NASB). A. W. Tozer wrote of God: "No one can dissuade Him from His purposes; nothing turn Him aside from His plans. Since He is omniscient, there can be no unforeseen circumstances, no accidents. As He is sovereign, there can be no countermanded orders, no breakdown in authority; and as He is omnipotent, there can be no want of power to achieve His chosen ends. God is sufficient unto Himself for all these things."*

Even in our lowest moments and despite unwise decisions, God's plans remain intact. He is watching over us and has set in motion everything that needs to take place to fulfill them. Remember Hagar? When she fled from Sarai, the Lord sought her in the wilderness and corrected her course (Genesis 16). After running for his life, Elijah asked God to let him die; but God sustained him through forty days of wandering before directing him to his mission (1 Kings 19). And for Jonah, who disobeyed the Lord's command outright, God "appointed a great fish" to bring him to his senses and back to His will (Jonah 1:17).

Through His presence, through circumstances, God guides us. "You have hedged me behind and before, and laid Your hand upon me," we read in Psalms (139:5 NKJV). So next time you begin to wonder, remember: God has good plans for you (Jeremiah 29:11), and nothing can foil them.

*God, You are awesome! Thank You for the certainty that Your plans for me will be fulfilled. Amen.*

---

*A. W. Tozer, *The Knowledge of the Holy* (New York: HarperSanFrancisco, 1961), 111–12.

# Apples to Oranges

*Make a careful exploration of who you are and the work you*
*have been given, and then sink yourself into that. Don't be*
*impressed with yourself. Don't compare yourself with others.*
*Each of you must take responsibility for doing the*
*creative best you can with your own life.*

GALATIANS 6:4–5 MSG

If spiritual gifts came with instruction manuals, they might include some words of caution. *Caution?* God's gifts are blessings; He uses them to equip His own. Where is the danger in something so wonderful? But if you've ever become bigheaded over your gift or belittled yourself because of someone else's, you know the importance of handling your gift with care.

Using our gifts carefully is possible only with a right frame of mind. No gift, no matter how big or small, is a result of human effort alone, since God is the one who gifts. We should see our gifts as products of grace, divinely apportioned by God. Paul advised believers, "For I say, through the grace given to me, to everyone who is among you, not to think of himself more highly than he ought to think, but to think soberly, as God has dealt to each one a measure of faith" (Romans 12:3 NKJV). Or, as The Message translates Paul's words, "Living then, as every one of you does, in pure grace, it's important that you not misinterpret yourselves as people who are bringing this goodness to God. No, God brings it all to you. The only accurate way to understand ourselves is by what God is and by what he does for us." And what God does—in His wisdom and love—is gift every believer individually. He has assigned each of us a one-of-a-kind part in His kingdom work, complete with a one-of-a-kind gift. Paul went on to say, "Each one of us has a body with many parts, and these parts all have different uses. In the same way, we are many, but in Christ we are all one body. . . . We all have different gifts, each of which came because of the grace God gave us" (Romans 12:4–6 NCV).

One God, many gifts. One God, many ways He works through us (1 Corinthians 12:4–6). How should we handle the gift? Peter wrote, "As each has received a gift, use it to serve one another, as good stewards of God's varied grace" (1 Peter 4:10). We, as the recipients, do our part with the gifts God has given us, no comparing allowed.

*God, like everything in my life, my gift is not random.*
*You've gifted me perfectly to fulfill Your plans perfectly.*
*Please show me how to use my gift for Your glory. Amen.*

# Going Home

*Jesus answered him, "If anyone loves me, he will keep my word, and my Father will love him, and we will come to him and make our home with him."*
JOHN 14:23

There's no place like home. When we're at home, we can breathe deeply, relax. We are secure. We belong. But sometimes even "home" can be uncertain. It may be month after month of struggling to pay the rent or mortgage that makes us question whether we'll have a place to live. It may be a natural disaster that rips our dwelling from us. If our earthly home was all there is, we'd justifiably despair. For the Christian, though, there's more. There's hope. This life is pointing toward the next.

Woven into God's Word is the truth that this earth is impermanent. The world as we know it is passing away (1 Corinthians 7:31; 1 John 2:17), and we are only sojourners on the planet. In fact, far from guaranteeing believers a sheltered existence, Jesus described a nomad's life in response to a scribe's declaration that he would follow Jesus wherever He went: "Foxes have holes, and birds of the air have nests, but the Son of Man has nowhere to lay his head" (Matthew 8:20). Jesus was just passing through, doing the Father's will until joining Him again in heaven. Once adopted into God's family, believers are also to consider this life a temporary residence, a perishable home that God will replace one day. Peter told pilgrim believers, "Friends, this world is not your home, so don't make yourselves cozy in it" (1 Peter 2:11 MSG). And Hebrews 13:14 (NCV) says, "Here on earth we do not have a city that lasts forever, but we are looking for the city that we will have in the future."

Our Lord is in heaven this very minute readying our eternal home. He told the disciples, "Let not your hearts be troubled. Believe in God; believe also in me. In my Father's house are many rooms. If it were not so, would I have told you that I go to prepare a place for you? And if I go and prepare a place for you, I will come again and will take you to myself, that where I am you may be also" (John 14:1–3). One day, we'll be going home. In the meantime, we have another promise—that God will make a home in us, preparing us for that day when we will be forever at home.

*Lord, thank You for a roof over my head. Even if that roof becomes fragile, I know You are with me. And I know You will have a home waiting for me in heaven. Amen.*

# What a Plan!

*Oh, the depth of the riches and wisdom and knowledge of God! How unsearchable are his judgments and how inscrutable his ways! . . . For from him and through him and to him are all things.*

ROMANS 11:33, 36

enturies before Israel rejected Christ as Messiah, Ezekiel, a prophet and priest, delivered a promise from the Lord to the nation: "And I will give you a new heart, and a new spirit I will put within you. And I will remove the heart of stone from your flesh and give you a heart of flesh. And I will put my Spirit within you" (Ezekiel 36:26–27). God's people will not continue on with hardened hearts everlastingly. One day He will replace hearts of stone with hearts of flesh and fill them with the Holy Spirit. It's part of the plan.

What plan? The plan to extend salvation to every nation. In one of God's inscrutable ways, He made provision for the Gentiles' rescue through Israel's rejection of Christ. Paul wrote, "So I ask, did they stumble in order that they might fall? By no means! Rather, through their trespass salvation has come to the Gentiles" (Romans 11:11). The branches broken off allowed others to be grafted in (Romans 11:17); Israel's unbelief opened the door to belief for everyone. We had unrepentant hearts before God called to us and offered renewal. Now God has transformed us through faith with hearts alive to Him and the indwelling Spirit empowering and guiding us.

But, as Paul warned, we should never let God's kindness swell us with pride because we accepted what Israel rejected. Israel's spiritual hardness of heart will last only for a time, until God's chosen among the Gentiles find salvation (Romans 11:25). Then God will redeem His chosen nation, His cherished people: "Concerning the gospel they are enemies for your sake, but concerning the election they are beloved for the sake of the fathers. For the gifts and the calling of God are irrevocable. For as you were once disobedient to God, yet have now obtained mercy through their disobedience, even so these also have now been disobedient, that through the mercy shown you they also may obtain mercy. For God has committed them all to disobedience, that He might have mercy on all" (Romans 11:28–32 NKJV).

God's plan is magnificent. "Oh, the depth. . . !" Paul declared. We could spend whole lifetimes contemplating how amazing our God is. "Everything comes from him; everything happens through him; everything ends up in him. Always glory! Always praise!" (Romans 11:36 MSG).

*God, I'll never fully grasp the whys and the workings of Your plans. They are too wonderful! To You be the glory. Amen.*

# It's a Tie

" 'Am I not allowed to do what I choose with what belongs
to me? Or do you begrudge my generosity?'
So the last will be first, and the first last."
MATTHEW 20:15–16

Six o'clock in the morning. The sun was still fresh on the horizon, and a full day's toil awaited, twelve long hours of working hard and bearing the heat of that sun. The vineyard owner had left his house and traveled to the marketplace in search of laborers. He now hired the first batch and promised to pay them a fair wage for their work, which they willingly accepted. Three hours later, the vineyard owner returned to the marketplace and saw others standing around with no work to do. He hired them too, but did not specify their wage, just that he would pay what was right. They eagerly agreed and left for the vineyard. Three more times, the vineyard owner went back to the marketplace and hired laborers—at noon, at three, and finally at five, an hour before work stopped for the day. When it was time to pay the laborers, the vineyard owner began with the last he hired—the ones who had worked only a single hour—and paid them exactly what he had promised the first—the ones who had been toiling for those twelve long hours under the sun. These laborers grumbled when they received their wage. Why should they—committed and hardworking as they were—not earn more? But the vineyard owner replied, "Friend, I am doing you no wrong; did you not agree with me for a denarius? Take what is yours and go, but I wish to give to this last man the same as to you. Is it not lawful for me to do what I wish with what is my own? Or is your eye envious because I am generous?" (Matthew 20:13–15 NASB).

The kingdom of heaven is like that, Jesus said. God, the vineyard owner, continually calls us to enter His vineyard and receive eternal life. Like the laborers in the parable, believers do not serve the Master on earth equally. Some come to Christ early and follow Him faithfully for a lifetime; others have only a handful of years or moments. But God does not dispense grace according to what we've "earned." He lavishly offers an undeserved full pardon to everyone who believes. So while the length and labor of our days are unknown to us—whether long or short, filled with toil or ease—eternity is equal. We all cross heaven's threshold in a tie.

*God, however long my life may be and however well I serve You, thank You for the promise of eternal blessing. Amen.*

# Unburdened

*"Come to Me, all who are weary and heavy-laden, and I will give you rest. Take My yoke upon Me and learn from Me, for I am gentle and humble in heart, and* YOU WILL FIND REST FOR YOUR SOULS. *For My yoke is easy and My burden is light."*
MATTHEW 11:28–30 NASB

What do you imagine when you hear the word *heavy-laden*? You might picture a mountain climber on her way up a steep slope with a backpack the size of a child. You might see yourself making one trip from car to kitchen with bursting grocery bags in each hand. You might envision a beast of burden lumbering down a road with a pile of goods strapped to its back. But when Jesus spoke of being heavy-laden, He referred to more than the heavy loads physically carried through life. He spoke of being spiritually burdened, of being weighed down and weary from the effort to live a godly life and gain heaven apart from God's grace. He came to offer rest and His yoke—the chance to slough off the old burden once and for all and to find new life through Him.

Jesus' offer was a marked contrast to the legalism popularized by the scribes and Pharisees. Of them Jesus said, "They tie up heavy burdens, hard to bear, and lay them on people's shoulders, but they themselves are not willing to move them with their finger" (Matthew 23:4). Their standards, the burdens they laid on people's shoulders, were impossible. Impossible to live up to and impossible to bear. So impossible that not even the scribes and Pharisees themselves were able to uphold them (Acts 15:10). Jesus, however, released people from the ultimate burden by bearing sin on the cross (1 Peter 2:24).

To receive Christ through faith means a cessation of endlessly, and futilely, working toward righteousness. It means rest in the grace of God. And it means an easy yoke. "Take My yoke upon you and learn from Me," Jesus tells us. When we take Christ's yoke, far from finding a demanding taskmaster, we find a gentle and humble Lord to guide us. We find a God whose commandments are not burdensome (1 John 5:3) and who cares about us so much that we can cast our burdens on Him (1 Peter 5:7). We find His very presence with us day by day, helping us shoulder the blessedly light load. We find rest for our souls.

*Lord, I was tired and burdened before I met You, but You brought relief from the heavy load I could not bear. Thank You for that soul-deep, abiding rest that comes only through You. Every day, I'll take Your yoke and wait for Your gentle leading. Amen.*

## By Your Side

*"It is the Lord who goes before you. He will be
with you; he will not leave you or forsake
you. Do not fear or be dismayed."*
DEUTERONOMY 31:8

~

Strength in numbers. If you want support, surround yourself
with friendly faces. How much easier it is to stand up for
what's right or to stand strong when you're wrongly accused
when you have someone to stand by you! But have you ever
been in a trying situation and all those friendly faces fell away?
What happens when you're left to stand alone?

The Bible chronicles the stories of real people who collec-
tively experienced the scope of real problems. You don't need to
search long to find examples of desertion. Even our Lord Jesus
Christ knew the sting of having the ones closest to Him shrink
back when given the chance to stand by Him. Just after His
arrest, His disciple Peter waited outside in the courtyard while
He was brought to the high priest, Caiaphas. Once, twice, then
thrice, Peter negated claims that he had been among Jesus'
followers—"I do not know him"; "I am not"; "I do not know what
you are talking about" (Luke 22:57, 58, 60). Seeing into Peter's
heart, Jesus would later forgive his denial; He would, in fact, ask
His Father to forgive the ones who crucified Him (Luke 23:34).
But that day, Jesus faced His accusers alone.

Paul also stood accused and alone. Near the end of his

ministry, Paul was imprisoned in Rome, likely a result of Nero's persecution of Christians. When he was brought before the court, nobody defended him. "At my first defense no one came to stand by me, but all deserted me. May it not be charged against them!" Paul wrote to Timothy (2 Timothy 4:16). Despite outward abandonment, though, Paul had faith that he was never truly alone: "But the Lord stood by me and strengthened me, so that through me the message might be fully proclaimed and all the Gentiles might hear it. So I was rescued from the lion's mouth. The Lord will rescue me from every evil deed and bring me safely into his heavenly kingdom" (2 Timothy 4:17–18). God was still with Paul, strengthening him and working through him to preach good news in bad circumstances. And because of God's present presence, Paul could count on Him tomorrow and always.

God will *never* leave you or forsake you. Whatever you're going through, even if it appears that you stand alone, God is standing by.

*God, I rejoice in You. I thank You, for You are a constant presence in my life. Though everyone might desert me— even those dearest to me—You will draw me close (Psalm 27:10). Amen.*

# At Peace

*Put into practice what you learned from me, what you heard
and saw and realized. Do that, and God, who makes
everything work together, will work you into
his most excellent harmonies.*
PHILIPPIANS 4:9 MSG

A few moments away, that's what she needed. A few moments to pause her restless thoughts. Lately her life was a jumble of discordant parts, a muddle of experiences and circumstances that had not yet blended into a melodious whole. Yes, just a few moments away. . . She turned on some music and closed her eyes. As the soothing notes filled her head, she remembered her God, thinking of all the ways He had been, was, and would be at work in her life. Jumble of parts notwithstanding, she sensed a deep harmony.

God's Word doesn't promise us that we'll know precisely what God is up to or how He will work things out in our lives. But it does promise us that in times of confidence and times of concern, we can have peace—peace that He is working all things together for good (Romans 8:28). How is that peace possible? Because it comes from God. Like the night Jesus said to the storm at sea, "Peace! Be still!" (Mark 4:39), only God can bring peace into our lives despite what's raging around us. Jesus told the disciples, "I have said these things to you, that *in me* you may have peace. In the world you will have tribulation. But take heart; I have overcome the world" (John 16:33, emphasis added). And the prophet Isaiah wrote of God, "*You keep* him in perfect peace whose mind is stayed on you, because he trusts in you" (Isaiah 26:3, emphasis added). When we mentally place ourselves in God's hand and wait and rely on Him for the order and purpose we crave, He gives us peace.

At the close of one of his epistles, Paul said, "Rejoice in the Lord always; again I will say, rejoice! . . . The Lord is near. Be anxious for nothing, but in everything by prayer and supplication with thanksgiving let your requests be made known to God. And the peace of God, which surpasses all comprehension, will guard your hearts and your minds in Christ Jesus" (Philippians 4:4–7 NASB). God is near, so tell Him, with gratitude for all He does, what's worrying you. His peace will empty you of doubt and fear while filling you with the knowledge that God is working everything together in perfect harmony.

*God, so much is unsettled in my life that I feel unsettled. I'm uneasy and uncertain. Please take the worry and replace it with calm. You are at work, so I am at peace. Amen.*

# Blessed

*Every good gift and every perfect gift is from above, and comes down from the Father of lights, with whom there is no variation or shadow of turning.*

JAMES 1:17 NKJV

ook around and you'll see them. Look up and down, right and left, behind and before, without and within, and you'll recognize God's gifts to us. His many blessings have His name written on them. The sun that warms, the rain that waters—*From: God*. The fruit and vegetables that nourish—*From: God*. The beauty of nature that delights—*From: God*. The companionship of others that heartens—*From: God*. The love and mercy that restore—*From: God*. And those are only a start. The psalmist said, "For the LORD God is a sun and shield; the LORD will give grace and glory; no good thing will He withhold from those who walk uprightly" (Psalm 84:11 NKJV). And John 1:16 (MSG) tells us, "We all live off his generous bounty, gift after gift after gift."

Why is God so good to us? Because He is goodness itself. "The goodness of God is the drive behind all the blessings He daily bestows upon us," A. W. Tozer wrote. "The goodness of God is that which disposes Him to be kind, cordial, benevolent, and full of good will toward men. . . . By His nature He is inclined to bestow blessedness and He takes holy pleasure in the happiness of His people."*

Our God is good. The scriptures declare His goodness,

verse to verse. "Oh give thanks to the LORD, for he is good; for his steadfast love endures forever!" (1 Chronicles 16:34). "I say to the LORD, 'You are my Lord; I have no good apart from you'" (Psalm 16:2). "Oh, taste and see that the LORD is good!" (Psalm 34:8). "Your flock found a dwelling in it; in your goodness, O God, you provided for the needy" (Psalm 68:10). "Truly God is good to Israel, to those who are pure in heart" (Psalm 73:1). "Praise the LORD, for the LORD is good; sing to his name, for it is pleasant!" (Psalm 135:3). "The LORD is good to all, and his mercy is over all that he has made" (Psalm 145:9). Our God is good, and as James pointed out, He will always be so. He does not shift like the sun, moon, and stars He created. Throughout the ages He has blessed us through His goodness, and He will go on sending blessings from above. Just look around and see.

*Father, You are so good; You are so good to me. Thank You for the blessings I see every day and everywhere. Amen.*

---

*A. W. Tozer, The Knowledge of the Holy (New York: HarperSanFrancisco, 1961), 82.

# Superfood

*How sweet are thy words unto my taste! yea,*
*sweeter than honey to my mouth!*
PSALM 119:103 KJV

D id you eat any superfoods today? Unfortunately, that *superb* mac and cheese does not count. No, superfoods are an exalted group of nutrient-packed, occasionally expensive, mostly tasty edibles that some believe boost health. It's the acai in your smoothie, the kale in your salad, and the salmon on your plate. They swoop in and fight the bad while nourishing the good. Yet whatever the superfood du jour may be, there is nourishment of another kind that has been around for ages: God's Word.

Moses had led Israel through the wilderness for forty years by the time he spoke the words recorded in the book of Deuteronomy. Along with the particulars of the law, Moses reminded the people how God had provided food. God's decree—His Word—that manna appear like dew each morning satiated Israel's physical hunger and directed His children to the source of spiritual fullness. Moses said, "[The LORD your God] took away your pride when he let you get hungry, and then he fed you with manna, which neither you nor your ancestors had ever seen. This was to teach you that a person does not live on bread alone, but by everything the LORD says" (Deuteronomy 8:3 NCV).

We see similar images of God's Word as spiritual "food" elsewhere in scripture. Jeremiah wrote, "Your words were found, and I ate them, and your words became to me a joy and the delight of my heart, for I have been called by your name, O Lord, God of hosts" (Jeremiah 15:16 NASB). And Ezekiel described his encounter with the Lord like this: "And he said to me, 'Son of man, eat whatever you find here. Eat this scroll, and go, speak to the house of Israel.' So I opened my mouth, and he gave me this scroll to eat. And he said to me, 'Son of man, feed your belly with this scroll that I give you and fill your stomach with it.' Then I ate it, and it was in my mouth as sweet as honey" (Ezekiel 3:1–3). The prophets did not actually eat the parchment and ink that displayed God's words; their ingesting was symbolic of taking in the Word and allowing it to work in them. When we study the Bible, chewing on its words and internalizing them, we experience lasting benefits. God's Word sustains us and grows us. It nourishes us. Even when the words are hard to digest, they are as sweet as honey.

*God, keep reminding me how important the Bible is.*
*I will eat Your words daily so that I am nourished. Amen.*

# Sweet Sorrow

*You have kept count of my tossings; put my tears in your bottle. Are they not in your book?*
PSALM 56:8

A coin has two sides, and so does this life. There is joy, and there is sorrow. We pray for more of the one and much less of the other because sorrow hurts intensely. We feel it through and through, like the sobs that convulse our whole body. We question *why us* and *what for*. While a cure-all answer doesn't exist, the Bible does assure us: God knows our sorrow, and He promises everlasting joy.

The prophet Isaiah used these words to describe the Lord: "He is. . .a man of sorrows, and acquainted with grief" (Isaiah 53:3 KJV). Jesus Christ did not experience just one side of the coin while He dwelled among us. Jesus felt deep sorrow and, ultimately, the anguish of the cross; He shed tears. Luke recorded Him weeping over Jerusalem's future (Luke 19:41), but it is John's short verse that most of us remember: "Jesus wept" (John 11:35). What's the story behind the verse? Jesus and His disciples were on the road, preaching and healing, when Jesus heard that His beloved friend Lazarus was sick. By the time He made His way to Bethany, Lazarus had been entombed four days. At the sight of Lazarus's sisters and the group that had gathered to mourn with them weeping, Jesus "groaned in the spirit and was troubled" (John 11:33 NKJV). And then He wept. Over their pain. Over the suffering that had its origin in the Fall. Praise be to God—Jesus saves us from our fallen state! "Surely he has borne our griefs and carried our sorrows" (Isaiah 53:4).

Psalm 30:5 (KJV) says, "Weeping may endure for a night, but joy cometh in the morning." Sadly, sorrow comes to us all, but we have hope if we keep our hearts trained on the joy that is to come. We find a glimpse of that future in the book of Revelation. John wrote, "And I heard a loud voice from the throne saying, 'Behold, the dwelling place of God is with man. . . . He will wipe away every tear from their eyes, and death shall be no more, neither shall there be mourning, nor crying, nor pain anymore, for the former things have passed away.' And he who was seated on the throne said, 'Behold, I am making all things new' " (21:3–5). In view of eternity, this brief life is only a night. God is hastening the morning.

*God, I am sorrowful right now. But You are catching my every tear, and one day You will wipe them away for good. Until then, be with me through the suffering; please bring me joy again. Amen.*

# Royal Wedding

*I promised to give you to Christ, as your only husband.*
*I want to give you as his pure bride.*

2 Corinthians 11:2 NCV

F rom the dress to the flowers, a bride spends countless moments preparing for the wedding. She's getting ready for her groom. Likewise, the church is getting ready for its Bridegroom: Jesus Christ. How does God demonstrate this relationship between Christ and His bride? Through the earthly example of marriage. Read these verses with that in mind:

> *Husbands, love your wives as Christ loved the church. . . . Christ used the word to make the church clean by washing it with water. He died so that he could give the church to himself like a bride in all her beauty. He died so that the church could be pure and without fault, with no evil or sin or any other wrong thing in it. In the same way, husbands should love their wives as they love their own bodies. . . . No one ever hates his own body, but feeds and takes care of it. And that is what Christ does for the church, because we are parts of his body. The Scripture says, "So a man will leave his father and mother and be united with his wife, and the two will*

*become one body." That secret is very import-
ant—I am talking about Christ and the church.*
(Ephesians 5:25–32 NCV)

Christ paid dearly (a bride-price, if you will) to bestow righteousness on us. Through faith, we are united to Him. He transforms us into a bride without spot, wrinkle, or blemish; He
cherishes us. Theologian Martin Luther wrote, "Who then can
value highly enough these royal nuptials? Who can comprehend
the riches of the glory of this grace? Christ, that rich and pious
husband, takes as a wife a needy and impious harlot, redeeming
her from all her evils, and supplying her with all His good things."*

One day a glorious marriage supper will take place. On that
day the betrothed will appear before the bridegroom. On that
day we will hear the shout, " 'Hallelujah! For the Lord our God the
Almighty reigns. Let us rejoice and exult and give him the glory,
for the marriage of the Lamb has come, and his Bride has made
herself ready' " (Revelation 19:6–7). Let the preparations begin.

*Lord, I'm thrilled that You've asked me to be part of Your bride.
I'm getting ready: staying true to the Word and readying my
heart for heaven, clothing myself in righteous acts—fine linen,
clean and bright (Revelation 19:8). I love You so much. Amen.*

---

*Martin Luther, *Christian Liberty* (Philadelphia: Lutheran Publication Society, 1903),
18–19, https://books.google.com/books?id=jv9EAAAAYAAJ.

## It's Personal

*The amazing grace of the Master, Jesus Christ,*
*the extravagant love of God, the intimate friendship*
*of the Holy Spirit, be with all of you.*
2 CORINTHIANS 13:14 MSG

If you've watched some rendition of Richard Rodgers and Oscar Hammerstein's musical *The King and I*, you may remember the lyrics to a song the character Anna sings: "Getting to know you, getting to know all about you. Getting to like you, getting to hope you like me." When we get to know people, it's personal. We learn and respond to who they are. In Christianity, the Trinity—Father, Son, and Spirit—is made up of three *persons*. Now, it might be easy to think of the Father as a person, and even easier to think of the Son as a person (He was flesh and bone while on earth, after all). But what about the Spirit? Maybe you identify with the words of A. W. Tozer: "The idea of the Spirit held by the average church member is so vague as to be nearly non-existent. When he thinks of the matter at all he is likely to try to imagine a nebulous substance like a wisp of invisible smoke."* Although it's difficult to wrap our mind around the Spirit, He is a person too, "endowed with every quality of personality, such as emotion, intellect and will. He knows, He wills, He loves; He feels affection, antipathy and compassion. He thinks, sees, hears and speaks."†

And we can get to know Him. The Bible tells us about the personality of the Holy Spirit. Here's just a sampling of His traits:

He aids believers (John 15:26). He thinks deeply (1 Corinthians 2:10–11). He comforts (Acts 9:31). He convicts (John 16:8). He guides (John 16:13). He feels and intercedes (Romans 8:26–27). He has power (Romans 15:13). He empowers (1 Corinthians 12:11). He dwells with us (John 14:17).

As we begin to think of the Holy Spirit as a person, He becomes more than a hazy doctrinal truth; He becomes a companion. Keep in mind, though, that the deep fellowship that Paul included in his benediction at the end of 2 Corinthians is a two-way street. Believers have a responsibility not to grieve (Ephesians 4:30) or to quench (1 Thessalonians 5:19) the Spirit—we grieve Him when we stubbornly cling to leftovers from our old nature; we quench His fire when we allow sin to kindle. But when we open our whole selves to Him, He will help us get to know all about Himself.

*Holy Spirit, You are not unknowable—You are a person! May You always be real to me, and may I never put distance between us. Amen.*

---

*A. W. Tozer, *God's Pursuit of Man* (Chicago: Moody Publishers, 2015), 69.
†Ibid., 72.

# Partners in Pursuit

*Keep on working to complete your salvation with fear and trembling, because God is working in you to help you want to do and be able to do what pleases him.*
PHILIPPIANS 2:12–13 NCV

❧

*S*anctification: a fancy name for God making believers holy. Once He adopts us into His family, God initiates the process of transforming us to be like Christ, a process that continues throughout our lives and accumulates with each successive day. While the work of sanctifying—the power behind it—belongs to God, we as believers are to pursue holiness in our lives with a healthy dose of respect (Paul called it "fear and trembling"). We are to keep at it.

The "keep on" of Philippians 2:12 (NCV) implies more than occasionally dipping a toe in the water. Our pursuit of holiness should be intently focused, methodical, dogged. Paul said of himself, "I do not run aimlessly; I do not box as one beating the air" (1 Corinthians 9:26), and "I press toward the goal for the prize of the upward call of God in Christ Jesus" (Philippians 3:14 NKJV). When Peter reminded believers of God's calling, he also used language that emphasized the immediate nature of seeking after holiness: "So don't lose a minute in building on what you've been given, complementing your basic faith with good character, spiritual understanding, alert discipline, passionate patience, reverent wonder, warm friendliness, and generous love, each dimension fitting into and developing the others. With these qualities active and growing in your lives, no grass will grow under your feet, no day will pass without its reward as you mature in your experience of our Master Jesus. . . . So, friends, confirm God's invitation to you, his choice of you. Don't put it off; do it now" (2 Peter 1:5–8, 10 MSG). While such a way of life takes effort, the benefits are twofold. Believers will have confidence in their salvation when they see the virtues they are pursuing manifest in their lives, and they will have an unimaginable reward awaiting them in heaven. Peter concluded, "Do this, and you'll have your life on a firm footing, the streets paved and the way wide open into the eternal kingdom of our Master and Savior, Jesus Christ" (2 Peter 1:11 MSG).

If the way you would describe your life right now doesn't sound like Paul's and Peter's descriptions but you wish it did, don't despair. Never underestimate God's power to work in you. He is already shaping your desires, and He will give you the ability to do what pleases Him.

*God, for me pursuing holiness has been willy-nilly. Please help me to live with more passion and purpose than I ever have before. Amen.*

# No Peeking!

*God has given them a desire to know the future.*
*He does everything just right and on time, but people*
*can never completely understand what he is doing.*

ECCLESIASTES 3:11 NCV

It was time! Her favorite part of the day was about to start. Teeth brushed, pajamas on, the little girl bounced into bed and snuggled under the blanket. "I'm ready!" she called. Minutes later, her father took his customary seat beside the bed, book in hand. "Now where were we?" he said, grinning, as he flipped the pages to the bookmarked spot then began to read. So lost in the fictional world was the girl that the sound of the closing book covers jolted her back to Kansas. "One more chapter, pleeease! I want to know what happens next," she begged. "No more tonight," her father answered. With a kiss on her forehead he said, "You'll just have to wait and see."

Our stories are unfolding each day. Don't you sometimes want to know what happens next—the specifics of God's story line for you? But in life, there's no staying up late to read a few more pages or skipping a few chapters ahead. We live sentence by sentence, even word by word.

This was the message Jesus delivered just before His ascension. By that point the disciples had a rough idea of God's earthly kingdom, yet they didn't know *when*. So they asked Jesus. "Lord," they said, "will you at this time restore the kingdom to Israel?" (Acts 1:6). Naturally, they wanted to know what was about to happen—"Lord, is it now, because we're itching to find out!"—but Jesus reminded them that some details of God's plan were not their prerogative: "It is not for you to know times or seasons that the Father has fixed by his own authority" (Acts 1:7).

We humans are often curious about the next page; God has purposely made us with eternity in our hearts (Ecclesiastes 3:11). God, though, is still sovereign over the *when* and *what*. Solomon in his wisdom came to understand this truth well: "I've also concluded that whatever God does, that's the way it's going to be, always. No addition, no subtraction. . . . That's so we'll quit asking questions and simply worship in holy fear" (Ecclesiastes 3:14 MSG). What God does goes. But remember: God is full of goodness and faithfulness. We can trust Him to do all things "just right and on time." We can worship Him in wonder of His mastery of all that is—as we wait for the story to unfold, without knowing what's going to happen next.

*God, I'm eager to see what's next in my life. Help me to rest in You, content that You know and control every page and the ending. Amen.*

# With All Boldness

*For God has not given us a spirit of fear, but of power
and of love and of a sound mind.*

2 Timothy 1:7 NKJV

❧

Let's paint a scene. It's ancient Galilee, and Jesus, newly risen from the dead, has gathered His followers on a mountain. The rocky, treeless terrain stretches out in all directions with patches of vegetation here and there. The wind whips the edges of their robes around their ankles. The sea is a gray expanse below. At the sight of Jesus, some break into shouts of worship for their Lord; others hold back, uncertain, wary. Then Jesus begins to speak. "All authority in heaven and on earth has been given to me," He says (Matthew 28:18). Right away, Jesus declares His sovereignty. "Listen up!" He was saying. "This is God speaking." Now comes the assignment: "Go therefore and make disciples of all nations, baptizing them in the name of the Father and of the Son and of the Holy Spirit, teaching them to observe all that I have commanded you. And behold, I am with you always, to the end of the age" (Matthew 28:19–20). From then on, Christ followers had an extraordinary commission.

Believers today still share in the holy task of spreading the Gospel. It's still our assignment. Yet how often do we relegate the job to someone else? How often is the greatest thing the least on our list of to-dos? How often do we let timidity stop us? Instead, we should follow the example of those first-century believers who took God's words seriously. In the book of Acts, the biblical account of the immediate aftermath of what we call the Great Commission, one of the first recorded prayers is a prayer for guts. Fresh from a round of the Sanhedrin's bullying, Peter and John met with friends and relayed the council's order to say no more about Jesus. The group responded as one: "Now, Lord, look upon their threats and grant to your servants to continue to speak your word with all boldness" (Acts 4:29). *Nothing* would stop these Christians from completing their assigned task. God's work was simply too great to keep silent.

Truly, God does a miraculous work in us when He gives us life through His Son. And never forget that along with this marvelous new life, He gives us a spirit to match—one of power and love and a sound mind. He uses us to spread the Good News.

Shout it from the rooftops!

*Lord, I know my mission—to tell others what You have done and are doing in me. Give me boldness to take Your message wherever I go. Remind me that You are with me every step of the way. Amen.*

# 100 Percent Pure

*How can a young person live a pure life?*
*By obeying your word.*
PSALM 119:9 NCV

❧

Sex is everywhere. Television parades it. Magazines advertise it. Movies flaunt it. Music puts it to catchy tunes. Books indulge in it. Even our clothing choice can shout about it. For the Christian woman striving for holiness in a sex-saturated culture, purity is an issue that must be addressed.

God created sex just as surely as He created man and woman. Within His design, sex is a blessing. But sin alters that design. Sin takes sex out of context; it takes a God-given desire and blows it out of proportion.

God's Word does not downplay the seriousness of impurity. When Paul wrote to the church in Corinth (a city that was filled with immorality much like our own culture), he emphasized both the danger of sexual sins and the weightier spiritual consequence: "Run away from sexual sin. Every other sin people do is outside their bodies, but those who sin sexually sin against their own bodies. You should know that your body is a temple for the Holy Spirit who is in you. You have received the Holy Spirit from God. So you do not belong to yourselves, because you were bought by God for a price. So honor God with your bodies" (1 Corinthians 6:18–20 NCV). God redeemed us. He sacrificed dearly to unite us with Christ. He paid a high price to make us

His living temples on earth, rescued from hell to glorify Him in heaven. We owe Him our all, including our bodies, and sexual sin damages us from every angle, bringing with it physical risks, an emotional toll, and spiritual harm. That's why God—in His holiness and love—sets the standard so high.

What is that standard? "But among you there must not be even a hint of sexual immorality, or of any kind of impurity" (Ephesians 5:3 NIV). Not even a hint. Nada. Nothing. And if we think the extent of purity is being chaste before marriage and faithful after we say "I do," we have another thing coming. Purity reaches all the way to the heart. What we watch, read, listen to, and think about affects us deeply and matters too. So how can we *possibly* stay pure surrounded by impurity? We must be on our knees and in the Word. We must ask God every day to saturate us so completely with His purity that there's no room for a hint of anything else.

*God, only with Your help can I be totally pure—mind, body, and soul. Shield my eyes and ears; guard my heart. I will be holy because You are holy (1 Peter 1:16). Amen.*

# Squeaky Clean

*Create in me a clean heart, O God;*
*and renew a right spirit within me.*
PSALM 51:10 KJV

inter, long and dark, had made its exit, and spring, promising and bright, had taken its place. Weak but warming sunshine cheered the landscape. Color flooded the world. Birdsong once again welcomed the morning. The woman opened the windows in her home, letting the fresh breeze spill in and fill every corner with sweetness. Then she got to work. Floor to ceiling, wall to wall, she began to clean: scrubbing the residue of the past, swiping dust that had been hidden by the shadows, bringing order to clutter, tossing the worn out, introducing newness. When she was finished, she surveyed the job well done and smiled. She hardly recognized the space before her, now as promising and bright as the spring.

Spring cleaning, the yearly rite of passage for homes, might not be as popular now as it was in our grandmothers' or great-grandmothers' day. When was the last time you hauled carpets out-of-doors or washed down every surface in your home come spring? But we still know how good it feels to have a fresh start—in our homes and in life.

God is an expert at giving fresh starts, an expert "spring cleaner." "Come, let us talk about these things," the Lord says. "Though your sins are like scarlet, they can be as white as snow.

Though your sins are deep red, they can be white like wool" (Isaiah 1:18 NCV). Before God begins to work in our lives, we are in need of a deep clean, but He takes those grody, sinful lives of ours and transforms them. He purges the old life and makes us brand new (2 Corinthians 5:17). John the Baptist anticipated the life-altering effect that God's Son would have as He cleaned out lives. The Message translates John's words, "I'm baptizing you here in the river, turning your old life in for a kingdom life. The real action comes next: The main character in this drama—compared to him I'm a mere stagehand—will ignite the kingdom life within you, a fire within you, the Holy Spirit within you, changing you from the inside out. He's going to clean house—make a clean sweep of your lives" (Matthew 3:11–12).

This cleaning house doesn't end at salvation. When God takes up residence in believers, He continues to remove gunk and replace it with holiness. Day to day He cleanses us from sin (1 John 1:9), day to day He cleans hearts and renews spirits—until that day when we'll hardly recognize ourselves in heaven.

*God, You've washed away my guilt for good,*
*and now You're cleaning up my life. Thank You! Amen.*

# Glory to God

*But we have this treasure in earthen vessels, that the excellency of the power may be of God, and not of us.*

2 Corinthians 4:7 KJV

A group of art students walked into a museum. They passed from room to room, pointing at one painting then another, nothing catching their eye for more than a moment or two. But toward the end of their visit they saw a painting that was like none other. Its brushstrokes awed them; its beauty enthralled them. "This painting is a master!" they exclaimed in unison. . . . Yes, those students had it wrong. The painting was a *masterpiece*, the work of an artist. Its brushstrokes, its beauty pointed to the painter.

Our lives as Christians should point to the One through whom we gain life—to Christ. His disciples knew this and were quick to redirect any misplaced glory during their ministry. Once, as Peter and John headed to the temple, they saw a lame beggar at the gate asking for alms. When he called to the two, they turned to him, but instead of offering money, Peter extended his hand, then healed the man in Jesus' name. This man who had never walked before literally leaped for joy. Crowds hurriedly gathered around Peter and John after witnessing the miracle and must have been gushing over them, because Peter said, "Why do you gaze at us, as if by our own power or piety we had made him walk? . . . It is the name of Jesus which has strengthened this man whom you see and know; and the faith which comes through Him has given him this perfect health" (Acts 3:12, 16 NASB). "We're only the instruments!" Peter could have said. It was God's power at work in a man who had no power of himself, not even the power to walk, that shouted "To God be the glory!"

God's Word compares our earthly lives to earthen vessels. In biblical times, clay pots were common; people used them every day and they were easily broken. We may wonder why our lives are like these plain, breakable pots. If God wants to declare His glory, why not make us shining golden vases? But God's glory shines brightest when He does miraculous things through jars of clay. Paul wrote, "We have this treasure from God, but we are like clay jars that hold the treasure. This shows that the great power is from God, not from us" (2 Corinthians 4:7 NCV). The pot that is nothing alone highlights the treasure.

These unfinished, fragile vessels point directly to the Master working through us.

*God, use this life of mine—this jar of clay—
to display Your glory. Amen.*

# He's Calling

*And those whom he predestined he also called,*
*and those whom he called he also justified,*
*and those whom he justified he also glorified.*
ROMANS 8:30

❦

The lazy summer day was winding down. The heat of the afternoon and the buzzing of cicadas were giving way to the cool of evening and a chorus of tree frogs and crickets. The young girl had been playing in her backyard kingdom for hours. Wrapped up in an imaginary world, she was oblivious of the passing time, of the cicadas and crickets and tree frogs, of the scorching heat or the kiss of cool as the day wore on. But then a sound caught her attention. She'd recognize it anywhere: the sound of her mother calling her name. Time to go in for the night.

God calls to us too. First Samuel 3, part of the Old Testament account of Samuel's life, is one memorable example. Samuel's mother, Hannah, had kept her promise and dedicated to God the son she had prayed for. Samuel, now an adolescent, had been assisting Eli the priest for years when he heard God's call. It was nearly dawn, and Samuel was lying down in the temple. Suddenly a voice broke the silence as the Lord called to him. Samuel, thinking Eli needed him, replied, "I'm here!" and ran over to the priest. Eli told Samuel, "It wasn't me; go back to sleep," and Samuel obeyed. The Lord would call twice more—"Samuel!"—and Samuel would rush to Eli's side twice more. On the second of these trips, Eli realized who was calling. He advised Samuel to lie down again and, if he heard God call, to answer, "Lord, I'm listening." God did call again, and Samuel heard the voice he as God's prophet would come to know well. So began a lifetime of Samuel listening and God guiding. The Bible tells us, "And Samuel grew, and the LORD was with him and let none of his words fall to the ground" (1 Samuel 3:19).

God's calling is a wondrous thing if you think about it. God determined, before the foundation of the world, the ones He would call; the ones He calls He makes right with Himself, and those He makes right He will one day glorify in heaven. Until that day, the Lord calls to our hearts like a shepherd to sheep: "He calls his own sheep by name and leads them out. When he has brought out all his own, he goes before them, and the sheep follow him, for they know his voice" (John 10:3–4). Truly, we'd recognize it anywhere.

*Lord, You called me to Your fold, and You call to me each day. Please keep my heart open to hear Your voice. Amen.*

# No Sole Souls

*Lift up a song for Him who rides through the deserts,
whose name is the LORD, and exult before Him. A father of
the fatherless and a judge for the widows, is God in His
holy habitation. God makes a home for the lonely.*

PSALM 68:4–6 NASB

Crazy, I'm crazy for feeling so lonely. . ." go the lyrics to the Patsy Cline song. Has your heart ever sung a country ballad about being lonely? Sometimes loneliness is more serious than a breakup, it's true. You don't have to be alone, either, to be lonely. You can be lonely in a relationship, lonely in the midst of friends, lonely in a crowd. But the Bible gives hope in loneliness. God's Word testifies of His concern for those without family (Psalm 10:14; James 1:27) and His care for those who are hurting (Psalm 34:18). And He doesn't leave any of us in our lonely state. He "makes a home for the lonely."

How?

*He adopts us into His family.* Once while Jesus spoke to a group of people, His mother and brothers arrived outside and sent a message to Him. Jesus' response probably surprised those who heard: "He answered, 'Who is my mother? Who are my brothers?' Then he pointed to his followers and said, 'Here are my mother and my brothers. My true brother and sister and mother are those who do what my Father in heaven wants' " (Matthew 12:48–50 NCV). As a Christian, you belong to a worldwide family of believers. You are part of a family tree that extends from earth all the way to heaven. Paul wrote, "So then you are no longer strangers and aliens, but you are fellow citizens with the saints and members of the household of God" (Ephesians 2:19). Reach out to your church family in your loneliness; God is making a home for you there.

*He assures us of His presence.* Moses' words to Israel just before they passed over the Jordan into the Promised Land remind believers of God's abiding presence through thick and thin: "The Lord your God will go with you. He will not leave you or forget you" (Deuteronomy 31:6 NCV). Wherever you go, whatever condition you're in, God promises never to leave, never to forsake. His presence is powerful enough to banish loneliness from even the loneliest heart. As you commune with Him every day and become aware of Him with you every moment, the truth is tangible—God has made a home in you (John 14:23).

That's cause for song, a song of praise.

*God, my loneliness lies to me, but I will believe You—I am never alone! Your people and presence surround me. Amen.*

# Please Who?

*The fear of human opinion disables;*
*trusting in GOD protects you from that.*
PROVERBS 29:25 MSG

~

Have you ever heard the term PK? It stands for preacher's kid, which is interesting but not what this devotion is about. Today you'll want to ask yourself if you are a *PP*, as in people pleaser. On the surface, being a people pleaser doesn't seem bad. What's wrong with tailoring your actions in consideration of someone else? Even Paul advised believers to please and not offend (1 Corinthians 10:32–33). But Paul also wrote, "Do you think I am trying to make people accept me? No, God is the One I am trying to please. . . . If I still wanted to please people, I would not be a servant of Christ" (Galatians 1:10 NCV).

Paul's allegiance was a choice, and it wasn't to people but to Christ—a one-eighty from his previous devotion. Before Paul became a Christian, he persecuted Christians zealously. Acts 8:3 says he was "ravaging the church." Then the Lord called and he followed. He left behind a life of pursuing the praise of his Jewish peers for a lifetime of serving his Lord and Master. He gave up earthly credit for eternal reward. He was imprisoned and stoned and mocked for Christ's sake without budging an inch. No one would ever say of Paul that he "loved the glory that comes from man more than the glory that comes from God" (John 12:43).

While on the surface people pleasing may seem harmless,

underneath we have our priorities reversed. Our first thought should not be whether people will applaud what we do, but whether God will applaud. Paul was all about being a God pleaser, and his passion revealed a heart aligned with God's. To the Thessalonians he wrote, "Just as we have been approved by God to be entrusted with the gospel, so we speak, not to please man, but to please God who tests our hearts. For we never came with words of flattery, as you know, nor with a pretext for greed—God is witness. Nor did we seek glory from people" (1 Thessalonians 2:4–6). Paul's motive wasn't self-seeking, as the motive behind people pleasing so often is. It wasn't to save face or promote himself; it was to do *God's* will. When he did "please people," it was with God and His salvation in mind: "I, also, try to please everybody in every way. I am not trying to do what is good for me but what is good for most people so they can be saved" (1 Corinthians 10:33 NCV).

As He did in Paul, God still works powerfully through lives focused on pleasing Him.

*God, show me where I'm pleasing people*
*instead of pleasing You. Amen.*

# A Certain Disciple

*Now there was in Joppa a disciple named Tabitha.*
ACTS 9:36

~

I n Greek, her name was Dorcas, which may sound funny to our ears but has a beautiful meaning: "gazelle." Tabitha was a Christ follower who is introduced in the book of Acts. We don't learn much about her; in fact, the biblical account of Tabitha takes up less than ten verses. But we can learn so much from her. Here's her story:

> *Now there was at Joppa a certain disciple named Tabitha, which by interpretation is called Dorcas: this woman was full of good works and almsdeeds which she did. And it came to pass in those days, that she was sick, and died: whom when they had washed, they laid her in an upper chamber. And forasmuch as Lydda was nigh to Joppa, and the disciples had heard that Peter was there, they sent unto him two men, desiring him that he would not delay to come to them. Then Peter arose and went with them. When he was come, they brought him into the upper chamber: and all the widows stood by him weeping, and shewing the coats and garments which Dorcas made, while she was with them. But Peter put them all forth, and kneeled down,*

*and prayed; and turning him to the body said,*
*Tabitha, arise. And she opened her eyes: and*
*when she saw Peter, she sat up. And he gave*
*her his hand, and lifted her up, and when he had*
*called the saints and widows, presented her alive.*
*And it was known throughout all Joppa; and*
*many believed in the Lord.* (Acts 9:36–42 KJV)

God worked through Tabitha's life in a big way, starting with small acts of kindness. She gave to the poor. She sewed garments. Tabitha wasn't curing diseases or preaching to crowds, but she *was* blessing others. And God would eventually use her to bring healing and tell of Himself. God raised His faithful disciple back to life, and the news spread—no doubt told first by those closest to her (some of the recipients of her good works) and then repeated throughout the whole town. The result? Many believed.

Our efforts may seem insignificant to us, only small ripples in the pond; but there's no telling what God will do through our lives. Would Tabitha ever have guessed how God would use her? God is able to take our everyday efforts and multiply them in eternal ways, ways we could never guess and may never know. He can take our faithful lives and make waves.

*God, You may never perform a miracle in me, as You did*
*in Tabitha, but You can always use everything I*
*do in miraculous ways. Amen.*

# What It Takes

*And he gave the apostles, the prophets, the evangelists, the shepherds and teachers, to equip the saints for the work of ministry, for building up the body of Christ.*
EPHESIANS 4:11–12

Fill in the blank: It takes a _____ to raise a child. If you answered *village*, you got it. The African proverb has become popular over the last couple of decades; it highlights the community involved in child-rearing—the family and friends and neighbors and professionals who surround a child and guide her as she grows. Now fill in this blank: It takes a _____ to raise a Christian. The answer? *Church.* It takes a church—more accurately, it takes *the* church—to raise a Christian. God designed it that way.

Ephesians 4:11 tells us that the Lord gave apostles, prophets, evangelists, and pastors. Why? To help His body—all believers—grow. He calls and gifts. . .

> to prepare God's holy people for the work of
> serving, to make the body of Christ stronger.
> This work must continue until we are all joined
> together in the same faith and in the same
> knowledge of the Son of God. We must be-
> come like a mature person, growing until we
> become like Christ and have his perfection.
> Then we will no longer be babies. We

*will not be tossed about like a ship that the*
*waves carry one way and then another. . . .*
*No! Speaking the truth with love, we will grow*
*up in every way into Christ, who is the head.*
(Ephesians 4:12–15 NCV)

God surrounds His children with a community of leaders—the apostles and prophets of yesterday and the evangelists and pastors of today—who equip us for service and guide us as we mature. God works through others to build us up and, sometimes, to correct us. One account of Paul and Peter found in Galatians 2 exemplifies this. When Peter stopped fellowshipping with Gentiles because he didn't want to look bad to the Judaizers, Paul opposed him. "Think about what you're doing, Peter!" he basically said (Galatians 2:14). Peter's conduct was damaging their message and leading others astray, but with some shepherding, the whole body was strengthened.

Who's your "village"? Through whom is God working to help raise you, His child? Think about the individual people—from pastors to teachers to fellow church members—whom God has placed in your life to speak His truth. Pray for them. Thank God for them.

*You have blessed my life with godly men and women*
*to guide me. Thank You, God. Please be with*
*them as they do Your good work. Amen.*

# Women of Our Word

*But as for me, I shall walk in my integrity;*
*redeem me, and be gracious to me.*

PSALM 26:11

We've all met her before—the woman who says a lot of good-sounding words but hardly ever makes good on them. She makes promises but doesn't keep them. She tells you one thing and then does another. She paints a pretty picture of herself that doesn't always match what you see. But while we can recognize her easily when she's somebody else, can we spot her in ourselves?

God doesn't take what comes out of our mouths lightly. Here's why. For such a little organ, the tongue has great power. James wrote, "If we put bits into the mouths of horses so that they obey us, we guide their whole bodies as well. Look at the ships also: though they are so large and are driven by strong winds, they are guided by a very small rudder wherever the will of the pilot directs. So also the tongue is a small member, yet it boasts of great things. How great a forest is set ablaze by such a small fire! And the tongue is a fire" (James 3:3–6). The tiny tongue has a huge influence. Our words influence our whole being. We should be careful of how we speak, especially when it involves others. We need to speak with integrity. Jesus told the crowds, "And don't say anything you don't mean. This counsel is embedded deep in our traditions. You only make things worse when you lay down a smoke screen of pious talk, saying, 'I'll pray for you,' and never doing it, or saying, 'God be with you,' and not meaning it. You don't make your words true by embellishing them. . . . Just say 'yes' and 'no.' When you manipulate words to get your own way, you go wrong" (Matthew 5:33–37 MSG).

There's another reason why God takes our words seriously. Ultimately, we are to reflect Him. We are to model His holiness (1 Peter 1:16), and He never twists His speech or lies or goes back on His word. He speaks with integrity: "God is not man, that he should lie, or a son of man, that he should change his mind. Has he said, and will he not do it? Or has he spoken, and will he not fulfill it?" (Numbers 23:19).

How's your verbal integrity? Do you mean what you say? "Those who deal truthfully are His delight," Proverbs 12:22 (NKJV) says. God is pleased when we speak truly. We have His Word on it.

*God, help me not to be careless with my words.*
*Each one has weight; may they all reflect You in me. Amen.*

## Bona Fide

*In this you greatly rejoice, though now for a little while, if need be, you have been grieved by various trials, that the genuineness of your faith, being much more precious than gold that perishes, though it is tested by fire, may be found to praise, honor, and glory at the revelation of Jesus Christ.*

1 PETER 1:6–7 NKJV

His friends hardly recognized him. His wife told him to curse God and die. Job had hit rock bottom, and the descent was swift. Just moments ago, or so it must have seemed, his life looked much different. Job had been rich—rich in family, wealth, and health. He had seven sons and three daughters. He owned thousands of head of livestock. His household boasted a large number of servants. He was the envy of his neighbors, "the greatest of all the people of the east" (Job 1:3). But in a bizarre sequence of events, Job lost everything: first the Sabeans stole the oxen and donkeys and killed some servants; next a fire burned the sheep and killed more servants; after that the Chaldeans raided the camels and killed yet more servants; then a strong wind leveled the house where Job's children were gathered together and they died. The final blow? Painful sores covered Job from head to foot.

What landed Job at the bottom? Nothing Job had done. He was "blameless and upright, one who feared God and turned away from evil" (Job 1:1). No, Satan—sure that Job's faith hinged on God's blessings—put Job to the test, and God—sure that Job's faith would withstand Satan's barrage—allowed it. Of course, God knew best. Job may have had low moments in the depths, but he came out with his faith intact because his faith was genuine; it was the real deal straight from God.

God's presence and working are behind the "In this" of Peter's words too. Here's how the New Century Version translates 1 Peter 1:5–7: "God's power protects you through your faith until salvation is shown to you at the end of time. This makes you very happy, even though now for a short time different kinds of troubles may make you sad. These troubles come to prove that your faith is pure."

When we reach the other side of trials still believing, still trusting God, we have proof of genuine faith. More than that, God refines our hearts through trials, removing the impurities like dross from gold. Unlike gold, though, true faith can never be destroyed, but only made purer.

*Lord, even when trials bring me to my knees, You bring me through, faith and all. Whatever happens in my life, blessed be Your name (Job 1:21). Amen.*

# Just Be Patient

*May the Lord lead your hearts into
God's love and Christ's patience.*
2 THESSALONIANS 3:5 NCV

❧

She tapped her fingers as she waited for her coffee to brew, then tapped her foot as she waited for her roommate to surrender the bathroom. She tapped the steering wheel as she crawled behind a slower driver on the way to work. She tapped her pencil as she waited for a colleague to return her call. More finger tapping as she waited for IT to fix her email, more foot tapping as she watched the cashier take *forever* to ring up groceries, and more steering-wheel tapping as she hit every red light on the way home. By the end of the day, she was tapped out!

If patience is a virtue, we could all stand a dose sometimes. Modern life just doesn't foster patience; we're used to high-speed everything. But before we decry modernity too much, we should remember that patience was an issue even in biblical times.

Paul frequently urged believers to be patient: "Therefore I, the prisoner of the Lord, implore you to walk in a manner worthy of the calling with which you have been called, with all humility and gentleness, with patience, showing tolerance for one another in love" (Ephesians 4:1–2 NASB). "Put on then, as God's chosen ones, holy and beloved, compassionate hearts, kindness, humility, meekness, and patience, bearing with one another" (Colossians 3:12–13). "Live in peace with each other. . . . Encourage the people who are afraid. Help those who are weak. Be patient with everyone" (1 Thessalonians 5:13–14 NCV).

Why did Paul push patience? Because he was well aware of the patience of his Lord. "The saying is trustworthy and deserving of full acceptance, that Christ Jesus came into the world to save sinners, of whom I am the foremost," he wrote. "But I received mercy for this reason, that in me, as the foremost, Jesus Christ might display his *perfect patience* as an example to those who were to believe in him for eternal life" (1 Timothy 1:15–16, emphasis added). The Lord did not tap His foot and say, "Forget you, Paul!" He was patient, perfectly so, and He is patient with us too. How often do we linger, yet He waits for us? How often do we sin, yet He bears with us? Truly, "the riches of his kindness and forbearance and patience" are meant to draw us to Him (Romans 2:4).

So what do we do? Let's turn impatience into prayer. Let's ask God to use each would-be impatient moment as a chance to display His patient heart.

*Lord, You have been so patient with me. How can I say thank You enough! Please help my heart match Yours. Amen.*

## Daily Dependence

*Our Father which art in heaven, Hallowed be thy name. . . .*
*Give us day by day our daily bread.*
LUKE 11:2–3 KJV

**A**re you a squirrel or a sparrow? Squirrels are the stockpilers, gathering enough nuts to last the winter, while sparrows are the scavengers, feasting each day on nature's provisions. In human equivalents, squirrels are the bulk-food buyers and sparrows are the daily marketers. If we're thinking of our stomachs, either approach has its perks. But what about our spirits?

Second Corinthians 9:8 says, "God is able to make all grace abound to you, so that having all sufficiency in all things at all times, you may abound in every good work." It stands to reason that if God will richly provide material resources, He will richly meet spiritual needs as well. He is able to give us every last needed drop of power, joy, peace, faith. . . But we cannot come to Him and expect a week's, month's, or year's worth of power, joy, peace, or faith at a time. D. L. Moody compared the Christian's need to manna: "I cannot but believe that the reason for the standard of Christian life being so low, is that we are living on stale manna. . . . The Israelites used to gather the manna fresh every day: they were not allowed to store it up."* How do we apply manna gathering to our lives? "If we would be strong and vigorous, we must go to God daily. A man can no more take in a supply of grace for the future than he can eat enough to-day to last him for the next six months, or take sufficient air into his lungs at once to sustain life for a week to come. We must draw upon God's boundless stores of grace from day to day, as we need it."[†]

It was this daily dependence on the Father that Jesus included in what we call the Lord's Prayer. He taught the crowds to come to God day by day for their needs.

And we can learn from the sparrow too. Jesus said, "Look at the birds of the air: they neither sow nor reap nor gather into barns, and yet your heavenly Father feeds them. Are you not of more value than they?" (Matthew 6:26). God promises to care for us. Why *not* go to Him every day for every need?

*God, how often do I fill up on You then go for days on my own, only to find I'm running on fumes? I need You every single day! Amen.*

*D. L. Moody, *The D. L. Moody Year Book: A Living Daily Message from the Words of D. L. Moody*, comp. Emma Moody Fitt (New York: Fleming H. Revell Company, 1900), 170–71, https://books.google.com/books?id=RQ6K3B8okAIC&dq.
[†]Ibid., 171.

# Looking and Listening

*I do not cease to give thanks for you, remembering you in my prayers, that the God of our Lord Jesus Christ, the Father of glory, may give you the Spirit of wisdom and of revelation in the knowledge of him, having the eyes of your hearts enlightened, that you may know. . .what is the immeasurable greatness of his power toward us who believe.*

Ephesians 1:16–19

Jesus was a master storyteller. The Gospels are dotted with His parables—from the parable of the prodigal son to the parable of the wedding feast; from the parable of the fig tree to the parable of the good Samaritan, and many in between. Why all the parables? There's more to it than an effective oratory style. Jesus tells us so.

The disciples wondered about Jesus' parables too. After Jesus told the first parable of His ministry, the disciples asked Him why—"Why do you speak to [the people] in parables?" (Matthew 13:10). Here was His answer: "To you it has been given to know the secrets of the kingdom of heaven, but to them it has not been given. For to the one who has, more will be given, and he will have an abundance, but from the one who has not, even what he has will be taken away. This is why I speak to them in parables, because seeing they do not see, and hearing they do not hear, nor do they understand" (Matthew 13:11–13). Rather than making spiritual truth clearer to those who do not believe, parables conceal it. Those with hearts hardened to God will find their eyes and ears closed to His truth. But to those who do believe? God opens eyes and ears and reveals His mysteries. Jesus concluded, "Blessed are your eyes, for they see, and your ears, for they hear" (Matthew 13:16).

God's gift to His own is understanding, and not just adequate but abundant understanding. "Those who have understanding will be given more, and they will have all they need," Jesus said (Matthew 13:12 NCV). To those to whom God gives, He keeps giving. As we read His Word, God uses His Spirit to bring sight and hearing to our hearts; He is helping us understand more and more of His truth according to His immeasurable power—"the utter extravagance of his work in us who trust him" (Ephesians 1:19 MSG). May Christ's command be our desire: "Whoever has ears, let them hear" (Matthew 11:15 NIV).

*God, thank You for giving me eyes to see and ears to hear; thank You for shedding light on Your Word and imparting understanding to my heart. Please be with me and work in me each time I read the Bible. Amen.*

# By Name

*He telleth the number of the stars;*
*he calleth them all by their names.*

PSALM 147:4 KJV

I t's one of the first things you're given. It's one of the first things you're asked. It's your name. Names are personal. They identify who we are: "I'm Liz." "I'm Ellie." "I'm Zoey." "I'm. . ." Someone knowing your name can make you feel special, set apart. You're no longer a nameless face among other nameless faces.

Psalm 147, a celebration of God's power and knowledge, tells us that our mighty God takes time to name His creation. "He telleth the number of the stars; he calleth them all by their names. Great is our Lord, and of great power: his understanding is infinite. . . . Sing unto the LORD with thanksgiving; sing praise upon the harp unto our God: who covereth the heaven with clouds, who prepareth rain for the earth, who maketh grass to grow upon the mountains" (Psalm 147:4–5, 7–8 KJV). Just think: the One who presides over the universe knows the stars by name!

And He knows our names too. In fact, often when God wanted to reassure His children of His care, He would remind them that He knew their names. The Lord told Moses, "This very thing that you have spoken I will do, for you have found favor in my sight, and I know you by name" (Exodus 33:17). He said to Israel, "Fear not, for I have redeemed you; I have called you by name, you are mine" (Isaiah 43:1). Describing Himself—the Good Shepherd—Jesus said, "The sheep hear his voice, and he calls his own sheep by name and leads them out" (John 10:3). And again the Lord said, "Can a woman forget the baby she nurses? Can she feel no kindness for the child to which she gave birth? Even if she could forget her children, I will not forget you. See, I have written your name on my hand" (Isaiah 49:15–16 NCV).

Our names are dear to God, forever in His sight and always in His mind. Possibly the least-favored parts of the Bible to read are those filled with lists of names. But even if our eyes cross and our brains lose track of all those names, God knows each one and the face behind it. He has compiled an even longer list of names too. If you are a believer, God calls your name, and He has written it in the Lamb's book of life (Revelation 21:27).

*God, You spoke the world into existence and yet
You speak my name. Thank You for knowing me
personally, for calling me to You. I praise Your
name, El Hayyay, God of my life! Amen.*

# Increasing Luminosity

*But the path of the righteous is like the light of dawn,*
*which shines brighter and brighter until full day.*
PROVERBS 4:18

They reached the overlook before dawn, inky darkness all around, and there they waited. First came just a shimmer along the horizon, a glow of color like a slash across the dark morning. But the brightness spread out and up, growing stronger. Silhouettes of clouds appeared as the sky became a wash of yellow to blue above the deep brown earth. Soon the sun peeked over the edge of the land, rising higher with streaks of light catching the mist. The landscape—once invisible under night's cloak—took shape as the sun rose, illuminated inch by inch from farthest coast to the grass beneath their feet. By noon, not a hint of darkness would remain.

Proverbs 4:18 compares the path of the righteous—believers—to a sunrise, which is faint at first but keeps getting brighter and brighter until it can be no brighter at noon.

What is the source of the light? God! The scriptures frequently tell of God's light. Notably, John wrote, "This is the message we have heard from him and declare to you: God is light; in him there is no darkness at all" (1 John 1:5 NIV). And David said of God, "For with you is the fountain of life; in your light do we see light" (Psalm 36:9).

Only because of God's light do we ourselves have light.

Jesus said, "I am the light of the world. Whoever follows me will not walk in darkness, but will have the light of life" (John 8:12). Before Christ, we are shrouded in darkness, so much so that we cannot see our way clearly to God. But Christ came to earth and shed light. He illuminates God's truth and takes us from the darkness of sin to the brightness of life in Him. "In the past you were full of darkness," Paul wrote to believers, "but now you are full of light in the Lord. So live like children who belong to the light. Light brings every kind of goodness, right living, and truth" (Ephesians 5:8–9 NCV). With light to guide our way, we can "learn what pleases the Lord" (Ephesians 5:10 NCV). And so our paths become brighter and brighter as we glow with increasing righteousness, as our hearts shine brighter and brighter with God's truth, until we can be no brighter one day in glory.

*God, You brought me out of darkness into light. Thank You for the promise that even when darkness floods this world, my path will only get brighter. Use Your light in me to light the way to You. Amen.*

# Sweet Dreams

*If you lie down, you will not be afraid; when you*
*lie down, your sleep will be sweet.*

PROVERBS 3:24

∿

**A**ll was quiet outside her four walls. All was still inside too except for her. She was tossing and turning. Left to right, back to stomach, she sought a comfortable position only to find a cramped arm or stiff neck. Hour after hour she waited for sleep, only to watch each hour tick by. . . .

Sleepless nights can befall even the best of sleepers. Who hasn't experienced, at least once, the frustration of trying to drift off to sleep and not being able to? And if sleeplessness is more often than not? Well, you've likely exhausted the entire repertoire of tricks to avoid spending yet another night staring at a dark ceiling.

Christians aren't immune to sleepless nights, but we haven't begun to tap, let alone exhaust, our resources until we turn to God. Philip Bennett Power, clergyman and writer of religious tracts, wrote, "Many a believer lies down, but it is not to sleep. Perhaps he feels safe enough so far as his body is concerned, but cares and anxieties invade the privacy of his chamber; they come to try his faith and trust; they threaten, they frighten. . . . There is a trial in stillness; and oftentimes the still chamber makes a larger demand upon loving trust than the battle field. O that we could trust God more and more with personal things!"* God isn't just hovering over the universe. He cares about us personally—noticing "every toss and turn through the sleepless nights" (Psalm 56:8 MSG)—and He is behind a good night's sleep. Psalms says, "He gives to his beloved sleep" (Psalm 127:2). Instead of tossing and turning, we can turn to the One who gives sleep. Instead of counting sheep, we can meditate on His Word. Instead of feeling restless, we can rest in Him. "They slumber sweetly whom faith rocks to sleep," Charles Spurgeon wrote. "No pillow so soft as a promise; no coverlet so warm as an assured interest in Christ."[†]

Next time you're lying awake in the wee hours, think of the psalmist's words: "He who watches over you will not slumber; indeed, he who watches over Israel will neither slumber nor sleep. The LORD watches over you. . .the sun will not harm you by day, nor the moon by night" (Psalm 121:3–6 NIV). Call on God in your sleeplessness. He's with you day *and* night.

*Lord, here I am again, wide awake when I should be fast asleep. Please calm my mind and relax my body; use this time to bring me true rest in You. Amen.*

*Charles H. Spurgeon, *The Treasury of David* (n.p.: Classic Century Works, 2011), Psalm 4.
†Ibid.

# Unexpected Joy

*Remember those days in the past when you first learned the truth. You had a hard struggle with many sufferings, but you continued strong. Sometimes you were hurt and attacked before crowds of people, and sometimes you shared with those who were being treated that way. . . . You even had joy when all that you owned was taken from you.*

HEBREWS 10:32–34 NCV

**W**hat on earth?! Imagine yourself as one of these Hebrews. You've struggled through one episode of suffering after another, faced ridicule and linked arms with those who faced it. Your property is seized, and how do you take it? Joyfully. As in, "I'm joyful, even though everything I possess has been plundered!" Not the reaction you might expect, but neither is it an isolated incident. Take, for instance, the time the apostles were arrested and beaten but "left the presence of the council, rejoicing" (Acts 5:41). How could the apostles and the Hebrews accept persecution with joy? The rest of the verses tell how: the apostles rejoiced "that they were counted worthy to suffer dishonor for [Jesus'] name" (verse 41), and the Hebrews "knew [they] had something better and more lasting" to call their own (Hebrews 10:34 NCV).

How can we look on trials as "pure joy" (James 1:2 NIV)? By seeing beyond the temporal to the eternal. By focusing on the ways tribulation prepares us for that better and lasting something.

"We also glory in tribulations," Paul said, "knowing that tribulation produces perseverance; and perseverance, character; and character, hope. Now hope does not disappoint, because the love of God has been poured out in our hearts" (Romans 5:3–5 NKJV). As we are being built through trials, we always and with complete confidence have hope because of God's work in us. Hope of what? Our inheritance in eternity—what Peter described as "an inheritance incorruptible and undefiled and that does not fade away, reserved in heaven for you" (1 Peter 1:4 NKJV). John MacArthur wrote this about Peter's words: "Peter showed those persecuted Christians how to look past their troubles to their eternal inheritance. Life, righteousness, joy, peace, perfection, God's presence, Christ's glorious companionship, rewards, and all else God has planned is the Christian's heavenly inheritance."*

Jesus once compared the kingdom of heaven to treasure hidden in a field. A man who found the treasure buried it and, joyful, went and sold all that was his to make the field his own (Matthew 13:44). With such joy do we anticipate heaven, so that everything on earth pales by comparison.

*God, when tribulation and persecution come my way, help me to meet them with joy. You are working good through them now and into eternity. Amen.*

---

*John MacArthur, *The MacArthur Bible Commentary* (Nashville: Thomas Nelson, 2005), 1904.

# Low Boiling Point

*Always be willing to listen and slow to speak. Do not become angry easily, because anger will not help you live the right kind of life God wants. So put out of your life every evil thing and every kind of wrong. Then in gentleness accept God's teaching that is planted in your hearts.*

JAMES 1:19–21 NCV

❧

"It makes my blood boil!" Ever said or thought that, or something like it? Truth is, lots of things can make our blood boil in life. Friends and family—though most of the time we want to wrap them in hugs—can make us want to fling up our arms in exasperation. Injustice and violence from Hometown, USA, to the other side of the globe can make us clench our fists against evil. And those are just cursory examples.

Since the causes of anger are so prevalent, we may be tempted to justify anger. Even Jesus got mad! One year at Passover, He went up to Jerusalem and, upon entering the temple, witnessed a scene that made His blood boil. Those who traveled to the city to celebrate Passover couldn't always bring sacrificial animals with them; they didn't always have the correct currency to offer either. So some merchants and money changers decided to profit from the worshippers' lack, selling oxen, sheep, and pigeons in the courts and charging fees to exchange money. Upset by the way these people were filling God's holy place with unholiness, Jesus drove them out, overturned the tables, and demanded they change their ways (John 2:13–16).

Anger itself is not sin. But unlike God's perfect Son, who knew how to be angry without sinning, we need to be cautious about anger. Ephesians 4:26–27 says, "Be angry and do not sin; do not let the sun go down on your anger, and give no opportunity to the devil." And Psalm 37:8 tells us, "Refrain from anger, and forsake wrath! Fret not yourself; it tends only to evil." As anger permeates our hearts, it pushes out goodness. Our anger leads to hate; it leads to vengeance, which is not ours. "Do not take revenge, my dear friends," Paul wrote, "but leave room for God's wrath, for it is written: 'It is mine to avenge; I will repay,' says the Lord. . . . Do not be overcome by evil, but overcome evil with good" (Romans 12:19, 21 NIV). Our God will repay—justly, perfectly. So take a deep breath! We can release anger from our hearts, freeing space for goodness instead.

*God, I'm so angry I could scream! Calm me down, please.
I want to let go of this anger and grab hold of all
the good that comes from You. Amen.*

# Heart Healthy

*Dear friend, I pray that you may enjoy good health
and that all may go well with you, even as
your soul is getting along well.*
3 John 1:2 niv

"Work to live; don't live to work" is the mantra of many who strike a balance between work and life outside of work, between laboring and enjoying the fruits of that labor. Work takes up a great deal of our time, and if we aren't careful, it can consume *us*.

Now shift gears to a different kind of work—working out. Do you exercise to live, or do you live to exercise? Keeping our bodies fit and healthy is important; with nine-to-five desk jobs, commuter lifestyles, and sedentary pastimes to cope with, we need all the moving around we can get! But "moving around" these days isn't a walk in the park. There are gym memberships, training regimens, fitness crazes. Working out can take up a great deal of our time, and if we aren't careful. . .

So what does the Bible say about exercising? Not too much. You might have heard one of the few verses, if not the only, depending on your criteria: "For bodily exercise profiteth little" (1 Timothy 4:8 kjv). To see Paul's point, let's look at the verse in context:

> *By telling these things to the brothers and
> sisters, you will be a good servant of Christ*

*Jesus. You will be made strong by the words of the faith and the good teaching which you have been following. But do not follow foolish stories that disagree with God's truth, but train yourself to serve God. Training your body helps you in some ways, but serving God helps you in every way by bringing you blessings in this life and in the future life, too. What I say is true, and you should fully accept it. This is why we work and struggle: We hope in the living God who is the Savior of all people, especially of those who believe.* (1 Timothy 4:6–10 NCV)

When ordering our lives, God trumps self—and spirit trumps body. Strengthening ourselves through God's Word and training ourselves for godliness yields health and blessings that last forever, while exercising our bodies only touches the temporary shell. Take care of God's living temple on earth—your body. Stay fit to serve Him. But remember to monitor your heart when you work out, and not just beats per minute.

*Lord, my life is only a mist, here and then gone (James 4:14). I want to be healthy, body and soul, but may I always put more effort into working out my heart of faith than my heart of flesh. Amen.*

# Soar!

*But they that wait upon the LORD shall renew their
strength; they shall mount up with wings as eagles.*
ISAIAH 40:31 KJV

~

S he mentally calculated her next steps, envisioned the days
and weeks ahead, and sighed. The point in her mind flagged
"You are here" seemed impossibly far from where she needed
to wind up. How would she ever go on?

We've all heard the advice, right? "Take it one day at a time."
"Put one foot in front of the other." But sometimes even that good
advice falls flat. When the days stretch endlessly and we're too
bone-tired to lift our limbs, we wonder where we'll find stamina to
keep going. For you, maybe it's a project at work. Maybe it's health
issues. Maybe it's difficulties with your child. Maybe it's paying off
your debt. Maybe it's a rocky marriage. Maybe it's unemployment.
Whatever it is you're facing, hear some biblical advice: don't go it
alone.

Paul knew what it was like to be brought to the end of himself.
In Asia, he faced such extreme circumstances that he *could not*
continue on in his own effort. Paul, though, recognized God's
hand even in those most desperate moments: "We were so
utterly burdened beyond our strength that we despaired of life
itself. Indeed, we felt that we had received the sentence of death.
But that was to make us rely not on ourselves but on God who
raises the dead. He delivered us from such a deadly peril, and

he will deliver us. On him we have set our hope" (2 Corinthians 1:8–10). Paul couldn't do a little himself and then depend on God for the rest; no, he had to depend on God wholly. He had to fall back on his God, trusting God to uphold him.

Where is God when another day or another step seems unbearable? Where He always is. With us. Waiting to support our weight as we fall back on Him. "Do you not know? Have you not heard?" Isaiah wrote. "The LORD is the everlasting God, the Creator of the ends of the earth. He will not grow tired or weary, and his understanding no one can fathom. He gives strength to the weary and increases the power of the weak. Even youths grow tired and weary, and young men stumble and fall; but those who hope in the LORD will renew their strength. They will soar on wings like eagles; they will run and not grow weary, they will walk and not be faint" (Isaiah 40:28–31 NIV).

*Lord, You can work mightily through me. You can lift me up like air under an eagle's wings. Be my strength, be my power so that I can go on. Amen.*

# Chew Over This

*But Mary treasured up all these things,*
*pondering them in her heart.*
LUKE 2:19

The day was an ordinary one until Mary received an extraordinary visitor. What had she been doing before the angel appeared? Was she absorbed in household chores? Was she thinking about her upcoming marriage to Joseph? Was she settling down for the night? Whatever it had been, suddenly in her ordinary day there was Gabriel saying, "Greetings, O favored one, the Lord is with you!" (Luke 1:28). Her confusion must have shown, because Gabriel told her not to fear. He had been sent from God to deliver an extraordinary message: Mary would give birth to God's Son. Now, Mary marveled at this news. She was a virgin—how could she have a baby? But Gabriel assured her that God could do anything through His Holy Spirit. And Mary? She said "Okay!" and offered herself as a willing servant of God.

From that ordinary-turned-extraordinary day on, Mary's life wasn't typical, and it couldn't have been easy. Even though Joseph followed the Lord's command and married her, Mary likely found herself on the other end of some sidelong glances and gossip. Fast-forward about nine months, and Mary delivered Jesus, following an arduous journey to Bethlehem. Depleted yet brimming with love for the newborn babe, Mary heard the "good tidings of great joy" (Luke 2:10 KJV) from the shepherds and "treasured up all these things, pondering them in her heart." God was working in her, and He was working in the world in miraculous ways. It was a lot to contemplate, a lot to cause her to wonder what God was doing.

Fast-forward about thirty years, to when Mary watched Jesus die on the cross. She must have wondered what God was doing then, but the faith that had prompted her to say "Okay!" to God all those years ago would keep her trusting Him in the darkest hour. The first verses of Mary's song—known as the *Magnificat*—reveal her heart of trust: "My soul praises the Lord; my heart rejoices in God my Savior, because he has shown his concern for his humble servant girl. . . . The Powerful One has done great things for me. His name is holy. God will show his mercy forever and ever to those who worship and serve him" (Luke 1:46–50 NCV).

God is still doing great things. Let's join the psalmist—and Mary—in pondering: "I will meditate on all Your work and muse on Your deeds. Your way, O God, is holy. . . . You are the God who works wonders" (Psalm 77:12–14 NASB).

*God, I worship You! Today and countless days ahead,*
*I will think on all the ways You are working in*
*and around me. Amen.*

## "My Pleasure!"

*"The LORD your God is in your midst, a mighty one who will save; he will rejoice over you with gladness; he will quiet you by his love; he will exult over you with loud singing."*
ZEPHANIAH 3:17

A father cradles his newborn baby, a delicate bundle wrapped in strong arms. With eyes of joy, he gazes at her face. For weeks (years!) after, he thrills at the chance to tell others of his child. A groom stands in place at the front of the church, shoulders back, back straight; but there's no hiding his eagerness. He radiates the elation he feels inside, the pure joy at seeing his bride.

Think about God, and your first thoughts might be of an almighty, majestic, supreme, sovereign being. Rightfully so. He is all of that and more besides. He is the overjoyed Father—holding us in His arms, beaming ear to ear, brimming with love—and He is the jubilant bridegroom—breaking into song over His beloved. He is a God who delights in us. His Word declares it over and over, as in these examples from Psalms:

- *"He brought me out into a broad place; he rescued me, because he delighted in me."* (Psalm 18:19)

- *"The LORD delights in those who fear him,*

*who put their hope in his unfailing love."*
(Psalm 147:11 NIV)

- *"For the LORD takes delight in his people;
he crowns the humble with victory."* (Psalm
149:4 NIV)

It was with joy in mind and not sadness, willingly and not begrudgingly, that our Lord died and rose again to give us life through faith in Him: "Looking unto Jesus, the author and finisher of our faith, who for the joy that was set before Him endured the cross, despising the shame, and has sat down at the right hand of the throne of God" (Hebrews 12:2 NKJV). And it is with joy and not cheerlessness, wholeheartedly and not half-heartedly, that He works in us today and will one day bring us into His presence: "Now unto him that is able to keep you from falling, and to present you faultless before the presence of his glory with exceeding joy, to the only wise God our Saviour, be glory and majesty, dominion and power, both now and ever" (Jude 1:24–25 KJV).

Whether you are soaring high or feeling down, praise God for who He is—the Mighty One who saves *and* delights in you. He is at work, and it is His pleasure.

*God, I can't believe it! You reign over the universe, yet You
delight in me. What an awesome truth! How awesome
You are! May You be my delight too. Amen.*

# Put into Practice

*As for me, You uphold me in my integrity, and set me before Your face forever. Blessed be the Lord God of Israel from everlasting to everlasting! Amen and Amen.*
<small>Psalm 41:12–13 NKJV</small>

nicholas Herman of Lorraine was a soldier until he saw a leafless tree in the lifeless cold of midwinter. He thought of how, come spring, the leaves and flowers and fruit would return, and he was suddenly aware of God's caring, powerful presence in the world as he had never been aware of it before. He converted and became a Carmelite monk, best known as Brother Lawrence and for a posthumous collection of his letters aptly titled *The Practice of the Presence of God*.

For the rest of his life, Brother Lawrence *practiced* being with God—he made a habit of turning his thoughts to God, of remaining in His presence. His heart likely joined the psalmists who reveled in God's company and called for others to join them: "Oh give thanks to the Lord; call upon his name. . . . Glory in his holy name; let the hearts of those who seek the Lord rejoice! Seek the Lord and his strength; seek his presence continually!" (Psalm 105:1, 3–4); "Make a joyful noise to the Lord, all the earth! Serve the Lord with gladness! Come into his presence with singing! Know that the Lord, he is God! It is he who made us, and we are his" (Psalm 100:1–3). Don't miss a key point in that last verse: we come into God's presence, but God is the one behind us. As

David wrote, "You [the LORD]. . .set me in your presence forever" (Psalm 41:12). Brother Lawrence also acknowledged the Aide behind his practice, saying that when a believer "is a little too much absent" from God, "GOD presently makes Himself to be felt in his soul to recall him."*

How would a seventeenth-century monk counsel us today? No doubt to do as he did: "Think often on GOD, by day, by night, in your business, and even in your diversions. He is always near you and with you: leave Him not alone. . . . Do not then forget Him, but think on Him often, adore Him continually, live and die with Him; this is the glorious employment of a Christian. In a word, this is our profession; if we do not know it, we must learn it."† Let's begin putting his words into practice.

*God, whether I'm at work or play, I can be with You in my thoughts. Nudge my heart when my mind drifts too long from You so that I return to Your presence. Amen.*

---

*Brother Lawrence, *The Practice of the Presence of God* (Mansfield Centre, CT: Martino Publishing, 2016), 24.
†Ibid., 33.

# Dig Deeper

*As newborn babies want milk, you should want the pure
and simple teaching. By it you can mature in your
salvation, because you have already examined
and seen how good the Lord is.*

1 PETER 2:2–3 NCV

She lovingly called it "the tome." She had first discovered the tome as a little girl at her grandfather's house. Back then the large book was almost too cumbersome for her child's arms to carry. Undaunted, she would heft it off the shelf each visit and admire the marbled endpapers and leather spine. At first she only studied the pictures inside, but over the years, she began to read the captions, then the text. Layer by layer she read, until she practically knew the tome by heart.

Peter, when describing God's Word, compared it to milk. Like infants hunger after milk, believers should have a desire for God's Word. Reading the Bible is one way we mature as Christians. As we drink the Word, God uses it to form us like milk fueling a baby's development.

The writer of Hebrews employed a similar image to warn believers who were languid and even falling away: "About this we have much to say, and it is hard to explain, since you have become dull of hearing. For though by this time you ought to be teachers, you need someone to teach you again the basic principles of the oracles of God. You need milk, not solid food, for everyone who lives on milk is unskilled in the word of righteousness, since he is a child. But solid food is for the mature" (Hebrews 5:11–14). Christians are "born again," meaning God gives us eternal life and we are born into His family. From our new birth on, we grow, and as we grow we learn through God's Word. We aren't supposed to live on the basics but to advance in spiritual knowledge—to eat solid food.

God's Word is rich and living. We can study it for a lifetime and never exhaust all it has to say. But how often do we stop at a sip when we should gulp? How often are we content with an appetizer when we should dig in to the meat course? If you aren't digging in, do so! Every sip and bite of the Word has the potential to work in us; just think of what deep Bible study can do. Not sure where or how to begin? Pick a book, pick a chapter. Read, then repeat. Read until the words fill your head, remembering that the One who wrote the words also whispers to your heart.

*God, be with me as I delve into Your Word.*
*Use it to grow me and develop me. Amen.*

# Unchanging

*"For I the LORD do not change."*
MALACHI 3:6

❧

*lux* is one funny word. It means fluctuation or change. Things and people can be "in a state of flux," and certainly this is true for Christians, who begin to change from the first moment of belief on. Before Christ, we are trapped in our sin; we are defined by it. "And such were some of you," Paul wrote following a list of unrighteous titles (like idolater and thief). "*But* you were washed, you were sanctified, you were justified in the name of the Lord Jesus Christ and by the Spirit of our God" (1 Corinthians 6:11, emphasis added). Once called sinners, now we are saints. God liberated us from our sin and defines us by Christ. He is making us ever more Christlike, transforming us "into the same image from one degree of glory to another" (2 Corinthians 3:18).

Unlike us, though, God remains sure and steady. With all the changing going on—through growth spurts and seeming dormancy, good days and bad—we can fix our hearts on the One who does not change. A. W. Tozer wrote about this immutability of God: "The concept of a growing or developing God is not found in the Scriptures. . . . For a moral being to change it would be necessary that the change be in one of three directions. He must go from better to worse or from worse to better; or, granted that the moral quality remain stable, he must change within himself, as from immature to mature or from one order of being to another. It should be clear that God can move in none of these directions. His perfections forever rule out any such possibility."* So while God is perfecting us, finishing us (Hebrews 12:2), He Himself is perfection. Perfect holiness, perfect wisdom, perfect love, perfect grace, perfect glory. . .

Perfect presence. "I AM WHO I AM," God told Moses (Exodus 3:14). The New American Standard Bible notes that the "I am" of Exodus 3:14 is "related to the name of God, *YHWH*. . .which is derived from the verb *HAYAH, to be.*" God is. Stretch your mind as far as it can go backward or forward in time, and even beyond that point, God is. He says, "I am the Alpha and the Omega. . .who is and who was and who is to come, the Almighty" (Revelation 1:8). What does that mean for us? In our yesterdays, todays, and tomorrows, and into eternity, we are never without the Unchanging One who is.

*God, You always were, always are, and always will be.
I bow to You, and I thank You for always
working in me. Amen.*

---

*A. W. Tozer, *The Knowledge of the Holy* (New York: HarperSanFrancisco, 1961), 49.

# Finito!

*And through Christ, God has brought all things back to
himself again—things on earth and things in heaven.
God made peace through the blood of
Christ's death on the cross.*

COLOSSIANS 1:20 NCV

**B**etter is the end of a thing than its beginning" (Ecclesiastes 7:8), and as Christians, we can say "Amen!" to that. Each of us began life apart from God. We were born into sin, and our sinful nature kept us at a distance from Him. We did not walk side by side with God in the garden but found ourselves outside its walls. And unless you are one of God's chosen people, the Jews, you also found yourself an outsider to God's working. "Remember that at that time you were separate from Christ, excluded from citizenship in Israel and foreigners to the covenants of the promise, without hope and without God in the world," Paul wrote. Then came a huge *but*: "But now in Christ Jesus you who once were far away have been brought near by the blood of Christ. For he himself is our peace. . . . He came and preached peace to you who were far away and peace to those who were near. For through him we both have access to the Father by one Spirit" (Ephesians 2:12–14, 17–18 NIV).

Because of Christ, none of us must remain outside; we can freely approach God and remain there with Him. Second Corinthians 5:18 (NASB) says, "Now all these things are from God, who reconciled us to Himself through Christ." And Romans 5:1 (NCV) tells us, "Since we have been made right with God by our faith, we have peace with God." Notice the past tense in these verses. God has reconciled us. We have been made right. It's a done deal. Without a doubt, we won't end the way we began when we place our faith in Christ.

*We are unfinished*—those words began this book and were true of every one of us. And as the book ends, guess what? They are still true! We are unfinished. God will carry on His work in us until He calls us up to heaven. But God did not leave the greatest work He does in us unfinished. Christ's dying words on the cross were "It is finished" (John 19:30). His mission on earth was over. Peace with God was a reality. Redemption was complete. Praise God for that perfect work on the cross! Praise God for the precious words "It is finished"!

*God, Your work in me isn't finished. Sometimes what You're doing in my life brings me to my knees; other times it makes me dance. But always I can stand strong in the truth of what You finished on the cross. Amen.*

# If You Liked this Book, Check Out . . .

### Unhurried

Ever find yourself yearning for much-needed down time. . .more time to savor life's simplest, often best blessings? Featuring more than 120 faith-filled readings plus inspiring prayers and scripture selections—from the beloved King James Version of the Bible—this lovely devotional will encourage you to spend unhurried quiet time in the presence of your loving Creator.

Hardback / 978-1-68322-599-7 / $12.99

### When I'm On My Knees

*When I'm on My Knees* has blessed more than a million readers since its 1997 release, and now it's available in a beautiful 20th anniversary edition! With themes like praise, forgiveness, healing, trials, love, God's faithfulness, and worship, Anita Corrine Donihue's encouraging devotional thoughts will touch all aspects of your life.

Hardback / 978-1-68322-484-6 / $12.99